Asymmetric Information in Financial Markets
Introduction and Applications

Asymmetric information (the fact that borrowers have better information than their lenders) and its theoretical and practical evidence now forms part of the basic tool kit of every financial economist. It is a phenomenon that has major implications for a number of economic and financial issues ranging from both micro economic and macroeconomic level – corporate debt, investment and dividend policies, the depth and duration of business cycles, the rate of long-term economic growth – to the origin of financial and international crises. *Asymmetric Information in Financial Markets* aims to explain this concept in an accessible way, without jargon and by reducing mathematical complexity. Using elementary algebra and statistics, graphs and convincing real-world evidence, the author explores the foundations of the problems posed by asymmetries of information in a refreshingly accessible and intuitive way.

RICARDO N. BEBCZUK is Professor at the Department of Economics, Universidad-Nacional de La Plata, Argentina. He holds a PhD in Economics from the University of Illinois at Urbana-Champaign. Since April 2003, he is the Chief Economist at the Center for Financial Stability, Buenos Aires, Argentina.

Asymmetric Information in Financial Markets

Introduction and Applications

Ricardo N. Bebczuk

CAMBRIDGE
UNIVERSITY PRESS

PUBLISHED BY THE PRESS SYNDICATE OF THE UNIVERSITY OF CAMBRIDGE
The Pitt Building, Trumpington Street, Cambridge CB2 1RP, United Kingdom

CAMBRIDGE UNIVERSITY PRESS
The Edinburgh Building, Cambridge, CB2 2RU, UK
40 West 20th Street, New York, NY 10011–4211, USA
477 Williamstown Road, Port Melbourne, VIC 3207, Australia
Ruiz de Alarcón 13, 28014 Madrid, Spain
Dock House, The Waterfront, Cape Town 8001, South Africa

http://www.cambridge.org

Originally published in Spanish as Información Asimétrica en Mercados
Financieros © Ricardo N. Bebczuk 2000

First published 2003

Printed in the United Kingdom at the University Press, Cambridge

Typeface Times 10/13 pt.   *System* LATEX 2$_\varepsilon$ [TB]

A catalogue record for this book is available from the British Library

Library of Congress Cataloguing in Publication data
Bebczuk, Ricardo N.
    [Información asimétrica en mercados financieros. English]
    Asymmetric information in financial markets: introduction and applications / by
Ricardo N. Bebczuk.
      p.   cm.
Includes bibliographical references and index.
ISBN 0-521-79342-4 (hc.) – ISBN 0-521-79732-2 (pbk.)
1. Finance.   2. Financial institutions.   3. Capital market.   4. Credit control.   I. Title.
HG173.B3913   2003
332 – dc21   2002045514

ISBN 0 521 79342 4 hardback
ISBN 0 521 79732 2 paperback

To my mother, Alicia, and my wife, Sandra.

Contents

Preface

There is asymmetric information in a financial contract whenever the lender lacks the necessary information and control on the borrower's ability and willingness to repay her debt. To the extent that she uses someone else's money, the borrower has an incentive to disguise the true nature of her project, to apply the funds to a project different to the one she promised, and to announce lower-than-actual earnings in order to reduce her financial obligations at the lender's expense.

As trivial as this definition may seem, asymmetric information has crucial implications for a wide range of economic issues at both microeconomic and macroeconomic level, such as corporate debt, investment and dividend policies, duration and depth of business cycles, development of the financial system, rate of economic growth in the long run, origin and propagation of financial crises, and amount and volatility of international capital flows. Many policy-related puzzles have been solved, the close nexus between macroeconomics and finance has been established, and economic and financial forecasting have become more precise thanks to this theoretical breakthrough.

The formal study of asymmetric information started in the early 1970s and since the 1980s it has been applied to the finance and macroeconomics fields attracting, not surprisingly, the attention of a great number of researchers and practitioners. By now, asymmetric information has become part of the basic tool kit of every financial economist, and its theoretical and practical relevance has been recognized with the 2001 Nobel Prize for Economics to the pioneers of the theory, George Akerlof, Michael Spence and Joseph Stiglitz.

The guiding idea of this book is to present the topics listed above in a systematic and pedagogic way, developing the concepts in three parts: Introduction (chapters 1 and 2), Corporate finance applications (chapters 3 and 4), and Macroeconomic applications (chapters 5–8). Although there are countless excellent papers published in specialized books and journals around the world, their mathematical complexity, combined with a somewhat hermetic economic jargon, makes them hardly comprehensible for readers without the proper technical background. Introductory and intermediate corporate finance and macroeconomics textbooks, on the other hand, devote just a few lines, if any, to asymmetric information. The book aims at filling the resulting gap by making these issues accessible to a broader audience without losing the necessary technical rigour.

The book is intended as required or suggested reading in intermediate and advanced undergraduate courses in economics and finance, and can be used as a reference for graduate students in those disciplines. It is self-contained and does not require previous mathematical knowledge beyond elementary notions of algebra and statistics. Basic concepts and notation are introduced in chapters 1 and 2, and the subsequent micro and macro applications build on them. As additional learning resources, I use a large number of diagrams and numerical examples and present recent international evidence on the topics discussed.

I want to express my gratitude to those who helped me during the stimulating yet demanding process of writing the book. My dear friends and colleagues Leonardo Gasparini, Walter Sosa Escudero and Arturo Galindo stood by me along the way. From my days as a graduate student at the University of Illinois at Urbana-Champaign, I want to thank Werner Baer, who generously encouraged me and supported the project from the onset; Andres Almazan, who, besides his brilliant classes on finance and asymmetric information, provided me with keen and detailed observations on the manuscript that greatly improved the final product; and Hadi Esfahani, my dissertation advisor, who gave me fruitful insights to help build the bridge from theory to practice. José María Fanelli also took the trouble to read the original and make a number of very valuable comments. Last but not least, my undergraduate and graduate students at the Universidad Nacional de La Plata, CEMA and other institutions in Argentina and other countries where I have taught over the last few years, detected several typos in the first drafts and acted as an enthusiastic sounding board. Of course, remaining errors are my sole responsibility. Comments, suggestions and inquiries to bebczuk@impsat1.com.ar.

Veronica Fossati and Florencia Jaureguiberry provided thoughtful and efficient assistance. From Cambridge University Press, I would like to thank the trust, effort and kindness of Marisa Barreno and Josep Mas i Garcia in Madrid, and of Chris Harrison, Pat Maurice and Ashwin Rattan in Cambridge. Neil de Cort, my production editor, and Barbara Docherty, my copy-editor, did a remarkable job.

As for me, I have accomplished my goal of writing the book I would have wanted to read. Sincerely, I hope the reader enjoys and learns as much as I have while writing it. I welcome comments from readers and I can be contacted on ricardob@1psat.com or ricardob@cfsargentina.org.

The publisher has used its best endeavours to ensure that the URLs for external websites referred to in this book are correct and active at the time of going to press. However, the publisher has no responsibility for the websites and can make no guarantee that a site will remain live or that the content is or will remain appropriate.

Part I   Conceptual foundations

1 An introduction to asymmetric information problems in financial markets

A **debt contract** establishes the legal rights and obligations for those who receive financing (**borrowers**) and those who provide it (**lenders**). Essentially, the borrower promises to repay the principal plus the required interest in a stipulated amount of time. However, beyond all legal provisions, the contract is compromised once economic considerations are taken into account.

In the first place, the intrinsic **uncertainty** surrounding any investment project puts the borrower's ability to repay in question. As significant as it may seem, this obstacle can be reasonably overcome by estimating the probability of full reimbursement and consequently adjusting the interest rate. The second hindrance, the borrower's fragile promise loyally to obey the contract, can be more difficult to surmount. An experienced observer will note that a borrower can attempt to disguise the true nature of a project or, once in possession of borrowed funds, divert them to other uses or conceal the true outcome of his investment. These issues are known as **asymmetric information** problems. Conflicts of interests will arise if these factors hamper the lender's profitability. The origin of these obstacles and their effects on financial markets are the issues that we will study in this chapter.

1.1 Economic characteristics of financial contracts

In order to understand the implications of asymmetric information on financial markets we first need to explore the fundamental relationship between borrower and lender. A financial contract will be written only if the expected profit of the lender and the borrower is equal to or higher than the next best alternative project. This is the so called **participation constraint** or **individual rationality constraint**: no rational individual will take part in an investment either with negative expected return, or with a profit that does not reach a minimum required level of expected return, determined by the investment opportunity that is forgone for this particular business. This minimum floor is known as the **opportunity cost** or **required return**. Let us look at an example using the notation we will employ throughout the book. We will suppose there is only one productive project, with initial investment $I = \$100$. One year later it offers two possible **cash flows**: if successful, $CF_s, = \$300$; if it fails, $CF_f = \$0$. The probability of success α_s, is 0.7 and the probability of failure

$\alpha_f = (1 - \alpha_s)$ is 0.3. The **expected value** EV of the project is:

$$EV = \alpha_s CF_s + \alpha_f CF_f$$
$$= 0.7 \times \$300 + 0.3 \times \$0$$
$$= \$210$$

Does this project satisfy the conditions for the writing of a financial contract? To answer this question, we need more information. First, let us assume that the **initial investment** is $100 and the required return r is 10 per cent. This indicates that a lender who finances the project through a $100 **loan**, L, could obtain a 10 per cent return by investing his money in, for example, government bonds or simply making a bank deposit. He will not lend money at less than 10 per cent; nor will the lender be able to charge a higher interest rate, since borrowers will arrange loans with other banks charging 10 per cent.

The project involves a risk for the bank because, if it fails, the entrepreneur cannot repay the debt and goes bankrupt, transferring CF_f to the bank. However, the borrower is not forced to use personal assets to pay for the capital and interest owed. This feature of the contract is known as **limited liability**. Under the simple case in which $CF_f = 0$, the loan's **interest rate** allows the bank to achieve its opportunity cost $(1 + r)L$:[1]

$$(1 + r)L = \alpha_s(1 + r_L)L + \alpha_f CF_f$$
$$(1 + r)L = \alpha_s(1 + r_L)L$$
$$1 + r_L = \frac{(1 + r)}{\alpha_s}$$

In the previous example, the resulting rate is:

$$r_L = \frac{(1 + 0.1)}{0.7} - 1 = \frac{1.1}{0.7} - 1$$
$$r_L = 0.57 = 57 \text{ per cent}$$

Whenever $CF_f < (1 + r)L$, the loan's interest rate will be greater than the bank's required rate of return, $r_L > r$. Given that the bank will participate in the project, let us see if the borrower is satisfied with the contract. Assuming the borrower does not use personal resources for funding, the project will be attractive as far as it yields any positive return. The borrower's **expected profit** $E\pi$ is:

$$E\pi = \alpha_s[CF_s - (1 + r_L)L]$$
$$= 0.7 \times [\$300 - (1 + 0.57) \times \$100]$$
$$= \$100.0$$

As the project satisfies the economic demands of both parties, we can then conclude that the project will go forward. It is evident that both the borrower and the lender *expect*

---

[1] This equation implicitly assumes that the bank operates in a competitive market where no abnormal profits beyond the opportunity cost can be reached. This means that the bank is able to just cover the cost of its deposits (left-hand side) with the expected revenue from its loans (right-hand side). Additionally, notice that we assume that the bank has no operating costs.

(as opposed to *obtain* with certainty) a profit, because financial contracts are claims on *uncertain* future revenues. The project's actual value will be either $300 or $0, and not the expected value of $210. Uncertainty, however, means that probabilities need to be assigned *a priori* to every possible result, and both lender and borrower rely on such probabilities at the time of deciding to enter the contract. Accordingly, even though it may look counterintuitive, they do not care about the effective outcome but only the expected one.

In this example, we have assumed that the bank and the borrower are indifferent to risk, that is to say **risk neutral**. The bank makes no distinction between a safe income of $110 and an uncertain income that can be either $157 or nothing, with an expected value of $110; similarly, the borrower will obtain either $143 or nothing with an expected value of $100. As opposed to risk neutrality, most individuals exhibit **risk aversion**, meaning that they would prefer a safe income over an expected income of the same magnitude. Conversely, the risk averse individual will take on the risky option only if he is compensated with a *risk premium*, that is, he will be indifferent between a safe income of $110 and an uncertain, expected income of $120, where the risk premium is the $10 extra income from the second alternative. However, for the moment we will assume risk neutrality because, as we will see, it is entirely possible to analyse asymmetric information problems without introducing risk aversion, thus avoiding unnecessary complications. In later parts of the book, we will give risk aversion a meaningful role in our investigation.

This contract is relatively simple to establish and analyse, since the lender knows for certain both the cash flows and their associated probabilities. The risk of failing is present, but the lender appropriately responds by charging a higher interest rate. If both the borrower and the lender have access to the same information regarding the contract, we say the agreement is realized under symmetric information. Here we examine a case where borrowers and lenders do not have access to the same information. There is **asymmetric information** in a financial contract when the borrower has information that the lender ignores or does not have access to. Although we will be more detailed later on, for the moment we want to identify the crucial factors surrounding the problem of asymmetric information. This asymmetry concerns the lender whenever the borrower can use this information profitably at the lender's expense, and is connected with the following circumstances:

(i) The borrower violates the contract by hiding information about the characteristics and the revenues of the project
(ii) The lender does not have sufficient information or *control* over the borrower to avoid cheating
(iii) There is debt repayment risk and the borrower has limited liability.

We can illustrate the problem with the prior example, presuming that (i) the borrower knows the true probability of success to be 70 per cent, but reports 90 per cent to the lender; (ii) the lender has no way to verify what the borrower maintains; (iii) as before, if the project fails, the loan is not paid. Based on this information, the lender charges an interest rate $r_L = 22.2$ per cent $(1.1/0.9 = 1.222)$, so that the borrower's expected benefit rises:

$$E\pi = 0.7 \times [\$300 - 1.222 \times \$100] = \$124.5 > \$100.0$$

and the lender's expected income falls:

$$EI_{Lender} = 0.7 \times (1.222 \times \$100) = \$85.5 < \$110$$

It follows that if the borrower had not misrepresented the information, none of the above would have happened. The importance of repayment risk becomes clearer with a counterexample. We will suppose that the announced probability of success is again lower than the real one, but in the worst scenario the cash flow is $CF_f = \$110$. In that case, the lender can recover principal and interest in any event, regardless of whether the borrower states the probability of success as 70 per cent or 90 per cent. In other words, *if the debt is safe, asymmetric information is irrelevant*, since the borrower is unable to rely on her limited liability.

Important lessons can be learned by looking at the problem more formally. Let us rewrite the borrower's expected profit and the expected income of the lender:

$$
\begin{aligned}
E\pi &= \alpha_s[CF_s - (1 + r_L)L] \\
&= \alpha_s CF_s - \alpha_s(1 + r_L)L \\
&= EV - \alpha_s(1 + r_L)L
\end{aligned}
$$

The bank's expected income EI_{Lender} is given by:

$$EI_{Lender} = \alpha_s(1 + r_L)L$$

The formulas reveal the potential conflict of interests that lie between borrower and lender. First note that $E\pi + EI_{Lender} = EV$: The contract establishes how the cash flows of the project are distributed between the two parties. If the borrower can conceal the true risk of the project and deliberately overestimate the probability of success, then $\alpha'_s > \alpha_s$ (in our example, $0.9 > 0.7$), the borrower will retain a larger part of the expected value. The expected value is:

$$
\begin{aligned}
E\pi &= \alpha_s[CF_s - (1 + r_L)L] \\
&= \alpha_s\left[CF_s - \frac{(1 + r)}{\alpha'_s}L\right] \\
&= \alpha_s CF_s - \frac{\alpha_s}{\alpha'_s}(1 + r)L \\
&= EV - \frac{\alpha_s}{\alpha'_s}(1 + r)L
\end{aligned}
$$

where we use the lender's income statement introduced earlier to define r_L (note that the bank determines the interest rate based on the declared probability of success, α'_s). The ratio α_s/α'_s is a good measure of the level of asymmetric information. The lower this ratio, the larger the benefit of the borrower at the expense of the lender. It can be easily seen that, under symmetric information, the announced probability of success coincides with the real one and the expected profit becomes:

$$E\pi = EV - (1 + r)L$$

Table 1.1 *Project properties*

	Before disbursement	After disbursement
Pre-determined project	Adverse selection	Monitoring costs
Choosing between projects		Moral hazard

The borrower appropriates the expected value of the project, *net* of the lender's required return. Because this profit is smaller than under cheating, there is a clear incentive to exploit the information advantage.

1.2 Forms of asymmetric information

Asymmetric information in financial markets can adopt any of the following types: adverse selection, moral hazard, or monitoring costs. A lender suffers **adverse selection** when he is not capable of distinguishing between projects with different credit risk when allocating credit. Given two projects with equal expected value, the lender prefers the safest one and the borrower the riskiest. In this context, those undertaking risky activities find it convenient to hide the true nature of a project, thereby exploiting the lender's lack of information. By **moral hazard** we mean the borrower's ability to apply the funds to different uses than those agreed upon with the lender, who is hindered by his lack of information and control over the borrower. As in the moral hazard case, **monitoring costs** are tied to a *hidden action* by the borrower, who takes advantage of his better information to declare lower-than-actual earnings.

Before continuing, we need to highlight the differences between these three types of asymmetric information. Adverse selection appears before the lender disburses the loan, in contrast to moral hazard and monitoring costs. In these cases the problem takes place after having conceded the capital. In adverse selection and monitoring costs the borrowers are assumed to have previously chosen the project, while in moral hazard they can opt for a different project once in possession of the funds. Table 1.1 summarizes these properties.

Adverse selection

To study the effect of adverse selection on the borrower–lender relationship, we shall use some simplifying assumptions. There are two types of productive projects, A and B, with the characteristics shown in table 1.2.

As before, I is the initial investment, totally financed with a loan L, CF is cash flow, and the subscripts s and f represent success and failure, respectively. Naturally, $(\alpha_{a,s} + \alpha_{a,f}) = (\alpha_{b,s} + \alpha_{b,f}) = 1$. Entrepreneurs are risk neutral. Supposing both projects have the same expected value EV:

$$EV_a = EV = \alpha_{a,s} CF_{a,s}$$
$$EV_b = EV = \alpha_{b,s} CF_{b,s}$$

Table 1.2 *Project characteristics*

Project	Initial investment	Cash flow
A	I	$CF_{a,s}$ with probability $\alpha_{a,s}$
		0 with probability $\alpha_{a,f}$
B	I	$CF_{b,s}$ with probability $\alpha_{b,s}$
		0 with probability $\alpha_{b,f}$

with $CF_{b,s} > CF_{a,s}$, which, given the equivalent expected value of the two projects, implies that $\alpha_{a,s} > \alpha_{b,s}$. In the case without asymmetric information, the bank will charge a different interest rate for every project type:

$$(1 + r_{L,a}) = \frac{(1 + r)}{\alpha_{a,s}}$$

$$(1 + r_{L,b}) = \frac{(1 + r)}{\alpha_{b,s}}$$

Note that $\alpha_{a,s} > \alpha_{b,s}$ implies $r_{L,b} > r_{L,a}$, that is, the riskiest projects from the bank's perspective are penalized with a higher rate. But, no matter their differential risk, the expected profit is the same for both of them, that is, $E\pi_a = E\pi_b$:[2]

$$E\pi_a = EV - \alpha_{a,s}(1 + r_{L,a})L = EV - (1 + r)L$$
$$E\pi_b = EV - \alpha_{b,s}(1 + r_{L,b})L = EV - (1 + r)L$$

Note carefully that the lender receives $(1 + r)L$ in both cases, which suggests that the higher interest rate charged on the riskier type B just compensates for that risk: although the type B projects are asked to pay more than A if successful, the probability of success – and, correspondingly, of repayment – is lower. Ultimately, the expected payment to the lender is the same under both types:

$$\alpha_{a,s}(1 + r_{L,a}) = \alpha_{a,s}\frac{(1 + r)}{\alpha_{a,s}} = \alpha_{b,s}(1 + r_{L,b}) = \alpha_{b,s}\frac{(1 + r)}{\alpha_{b,s}} = 1 + r$$

It is also noteworthy that this means that, as long as we do not know the repayment risk of a particular firm, we are unable to assert if such a firm is facing worse financial conditions than others just by looking at the interest rate demanded on its loans.

Things change if the lender experiences adverse selection. Type B entrepreneurs have an incentive to 'camouflage' themselves to appear like those of type A and get the same low interest rates. On the other hand, the lender, though knowing the characteristics of each type of project, is incapable of observing to which type the entrepreneur pertains when seeking financing. The lender's only piece of information is the proportion of existing projects of

---

[2] This is a consequence of the competitive nature of the lenders' market, as no lender can charge an interest rate yielding an expected return higher than r. Also, bear in mind that the higher interest rate on the riskier projects does not constitute a risk premium but just the compensation for the lower repayment risk (since the lender is risk neutral, it requires a return equal to r on both types).

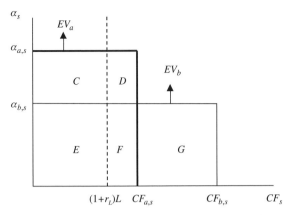

Figure 1.1 Distribution of EV under adverse selection

type A and B in the population, p_a and p_b, with $p_a + p_b = 1$, which allows her to infer that the probability of choosing randomly A or B is precisely p_a and p_b.[3] Provided that all entrepreneurs claim to be type A and the lender is unable to ascertain this, she will use these probabilities to establish a *single* interest rate for both types of projects in order to secure an expected return r:

$$(1+r) = p_a[\alpha_{a,s}(1+r_L)] + p_b[\alpha_{b,s}(1+r_L)]$$
$$(1+r) = [p_a\alpha_{a,s} + p_b\alpha_{b,s}](1+r_L)$$
$$(1+r_L) = \frac{(1+r)}{p_s}$$

where $p_s = p_a\alpha_{a,s} + p_b\alpha_{b,s}$ is the weighted probability of success anticipated by the lender. As $\alpha_{a,s} > p_s > \alpha_{b,s}$, the new, unique interest rate is an intermediate value between the rates that would prevail in absence of asymmetric information:

$$r_{L,b} > r_L > r_{L,a}$$

Type B borrowers' strategy is therefore partially successful, since they achieve a reduction in their financing costs but they do not get the looked-for rate $r_{L,a}$. Meanwhile type A borrowers suffer an increase in their interest rates, which is precisely what makes it possible for type B borrowers to reap an extra profit, as we shall see later. Combining the fact that the contract is more attractive for risky borrowers than for safe ones, the lender is prone to make an *adverse selection*, leaning toward the projects that are *a priori* less favorable for her interests.

Figure 1.1 illustrates the problem.

As the vertical axis represents the probability of success and the horizontal the corresponding cash flow, the rectangles $(C + D + E + F)$ and $(E + F + G)$ represent the expected

---

[3] This is an application of the statistical law of large numbers. If the lender knows that among the, say, 10,000 candidates soliciting credit, there are 7,000 of type A and 3,000 of type B, he can trust that a randomly picked borrower will be type A with a probability 0.7 and a type B with probability 0.3.

Table 1.3 *Distribution of the expected value of projects A and B*

	Borrower	Lender	Total
Project A	$D + F$	$C + E$	$EV_a = C + D + E + F$
Project B	$F + G$	E	$EV_b = E + F + G$

Table 1.4 *How outcomes vary with the existence of adverse selection*

	Project A	Project B
CF_s	300	700
CF_f	0	0
α_s	0.7	0.3
α_f	0.3	0.7
EV	210	210
I	100	100
r	0.1	0.1
p	0.5	0.5
Without adverse selection:		
r_L	0.57	2.67
$E\pi$	100	100
EI_{Lender}	110	110
With adverse selection:		
r_L	1.2	1.2
$E\pi$	56	144
EI_{Lender}	154	66

value of projects A and B, respectively. Knowing that project A has a higher probability of success, but that both have the same expected value, rectangle EV_a is taller with a shorter base than EV_b. In both cases, the cash flow in the favourable scenario exceeds the amount of the debt and interest payments, $(1 + r_L)L$.

As stated in the contract, the lender receives a fixed revenue, $(1 + r_L)L$, weighted by the project's probability of success, which yields an expected income of $(C + E)$ for project A, and E for project B. The type A borrower receives the remaining part of EV_a, $(D + F)$, while the area $(F + G)$ corresponds to the type B borrower (table 1.3).

As $EV_a = EV_b$, $C + D + E + F = E + F + G$, which implies that $C + D = G$. Hence, we deduce that $G > D$, or, equally, $F + G > D + F$, confirming that a type B borrower's expected benefit exceeds that of a type A borrower.[4]

Table 1.4 presents a numerical example that should reinforce the understanding of the idea and fix the notation.

---

[4] To observe the distribution of the expected value in absence of adverse selection, we can modify the chart by eliminating $(1 + r_L)L$ and replacing it by lines specific to each project; that is, $(1 + r_{L,a})L$ to the left and $(1 + r_{L,b})L$ to the right, recalling that $r_{L,b} > r_L > r_{L,a}$.

Table 1.3 shows how outcomes vary depending on the existence of adverse selection.[5] In absence of adverse selection: (a) the interest rate for risky projects is greater than for those with a higher probability of repayment; (b) independently of the project type, the lender obtains the required return r on each dollar or pound lent, while the borrower receives the remaining part of the expected value. The situation changes radically under adverse selection: (a) the interest rate is the same for both projects, specifically an average of the rates without adverse selection; (b) the lender's expected return is higher than the required return in project A and less than the required return in project B but, on average, the lender gets the required return. Consequently, the risky borrower obtains a larger benefit when there is imperfect information, with the opposite, naturally, happening for a type A borrower.

Moral hazard

We say there is moral hazard when the debtor invests in a different project than the one that was agreed upon with the lender. Let us suppose there are two projects, H and L, with the following expected values:

$$EV_h = \alpha_{h,s} CF_{h,s}$$

$$EV_l = \alpha_{l,s} CF_{l,s}$$

with $EV_h > EV_l$ – that is why we term them H and L (for high and low). We will also assume that $CF_{l,s} > CF_{h,s}$ and $\alpha_{h,s} > \alpha_{l,s}$. If the project succeeds, the loan is repaid, while in a negative event, the cash flow is zero. Regardless of the final use of the funds, every prospective borrower will announce that she will undertake type H projects, since in that way she will be charged $r_{L,h}$, which is lower than $r_{L,l}$. If the borrower, hiding the real type from the lender, embarks on project L, the lender will get an expected return lower than the required one. In light of that, unlike the case of adverse selection, as the borrower can choose the project in which the capital is invested, the lender needs to make sure that project H is more attractive than project L in the borrower's eyes. Thus, by ensuring that $E\pi_h > E\pi_l$ (the so-called **incentive compatibility constraint**), the interest rate will be $r_L = r_{L,h}$:

$$1 + r_L = 1 + r_{L,h} = \frac{1+r}{\alpha_{h,s}}$$

However, for this situation to be an equilibrium in which the lender as well as the borrower have the correct incentives to participate in project H, it is essential that the loan interest rate r_L is such that:

$$E\pi_h = \alpha_{h,s}[CF_{h,s} - (1+r_L)L] > E\pi_l = \alpha_{l,s}[CF_{l,s} - (1+r_L)L]$$

from which we can extract the *maximum* interest rate consistent with $E\pi_h > E\pi_l$:

$$(1+r_L)_{max} < \frac{\alpha_{h,s}CF_{h,s} - \alpha_{l,s}CF_{l,s}}{(\alpha_{h,s} - \alpha_{l,s})L}$$

---

[5] Note that the example is not very realistic, as the interest rates are exorbitant as a consequence of the high risk of the projects: not only are probabilities of success low, but also in the case of failure the lender does not get a cent. To make up for this, the lender takes possession of an important portion of the income in case of success by means of a high interest rate.

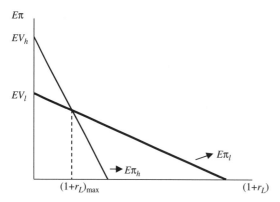

Figure 1.2   Project selection under moral hazard

According to this formula, the tolerance of project H to the interest rate increases with its expected value, but decreases with its probability of repayment. If $(1 + r_{L,h})$ is less than this limit, the asymmetric information problem will be irrelevant, as borrowers have no incentive to break the promise of taking on project H, and the lender will receive the expected return r. Conversely, a rate $(1 + r_{L,h})$ higher than $(1 + r_L)_{max}$ will attract all borrowers to type L projects, under the false pretence of choosing type H ones, in order to benefit from the lower available interest rate.[6] We can show this by observing the trajectory of the expected benefit as the interest rate rises (figure 1.2).

$$E\pi_h = EV_h - \alpha_{h,s}(1 + r_L)L$$
$$E\pi_l = EV_l - \alpha_{l,s}(1 + r_L)L$$

When $(1 + r_L) = 0$, the expected benefit is equal to the project's expected value, falling gradually until reaching the rate $(1 + r_L)_{max}$, after which $E\pi_h < E\pi_l$. The cause of the rapid fall of $E\pi_h$ compared to $E\pi_l$ is, once again, the structure of the debt contract: *for the same interest rate, the higher the probability of repayment (that is, the lower the repayment risk), the lower the borrower's limited responsibility.*[7] In other words, for type H borrowers it is more difficult to elude their financial obligations. To illustrate the point, let us observe how the debt service (capital of $100 plus interest) changes when the interest rate rises from 20 per cent to 30 per cent and $\alpha_{a,s} = 0.7$ and $\alpha_{b,s} = 0.3$ (table 1.5).

It can be seen that type H's expected profit suffers the most. Let us now verify with a numerical example that the expected value of the project is not the only decision variable at the time of choosing the most profitable project from the borrower's point of

---

[6] Notice how different the lender's attitude is in the face of adverse selection and moral hazard: in the first situation, as the borrower sticks to the original project, it is feasible to set a higher interest rate for type A entrepreneurs, while under moral hazard the ability of the borrower to switch between projects forces the lender to set an interest rate as low as possible to indirectly control the borrower.

[7] In the case of adverse selection, the problem is more acute because both projects are assumed to have the same expected value EV, which means that the project with a lower probability of repayment will always be preferred if the debtor is able to choose the project type.

Table 1.5 *Changes in debt service*

Borrower type	$r_L = 20\%$	$r_L = 30\%$	Difference
Type H	84	91	7
Type L	36	39	3

Table 1.6 *Decision variables*

	Project H	Project L
CF_s	200	400
CF_f	0	0
α_s	0.7	0.3
α_f	0.3	0.7
EV	140	120
J	100	100
r	0.1	0.1

view (table 1.6).

$$(1 + r_L)_{\text{max}} < \frac{\$140 - \$120}{(0.7 - 0.3) \times \$100} = 0.5$$

As $(1 + r_L)$ is necessarily greater than 0.5, the borrower will prefer project L, even though the expected value of project H is much higher than that of project L. Let us now imagine that $CF_{h,s} = \$265$ and $EV_h = \$185.5$, in which case the entrepreneur will choose project H, provided the interest rate does not exceed the following limit:

$$(1 + r_L)_{\text{max}} < \frac{\$185.5 - \$120}{(0.7 - 0.3) \times \$100} = 1.6375$$

The interest rate on project H is 57.1 per cent ($1.1/0.7 = 1.571$). Observe how wide the difference in expected value must be for the project H to be accepted in this particular example. Furthermore, if the required return r rises, not even this difference is sufficient. If r goes from 10 per cent to 15 per cent, elevating $r_{L,h}$ to 64.3 per cent ($1.15/0.7 = 1.643$), this again pushes the balance in favour of the risky project.

Much like the interest rate, the incentive to adopt riskier projects grows with the amount of debt L. It can be seen that the graph in figure 1.2 would look the same if we were to replace $(1 + r_L)$ by L on the horizontal axis. This finding should not surprise us because it is in line with our previous discussion: in the end, the temptation to dishonesty increases with the total amount of debt owed, including both capital and interest.

Monitoring costs

If the borrower takes advantage of his better information to deceive the lender by deliberately underreporting profits, the lender, who cannot directly observe the investment outcome, will be forced to monitor the borrower every time he declares himself unable to repay the whole debt. To do this, the contract stipulates that every time this borrower announces default, the lender has the right to audit the borrower and seize the whole verified cash flow. Every audit has cost c, devoted to hiring accountants and lawyers to do the job. For reasons explained later, we suppose there are three (instead of two) possible states described by:

$$CF_3 > CF_2 > (1 + r)L > CF_1$$

and the associated probabilities are α_1, α_2 and α_3, with $\alpha_1 + \alpha_2 + \alpha_3 = 1$. The lender knows both cash flows and probabilities, but has no information about the borrower's honesty. The possibility that the bank may seize the revenues at any time will prevent the borrower from declaring CF_1 when the true cash flow is CF_2 or CF_3. At the same time, declaring CF_2 when the actual value is CF_3 is irrelevant from the bank's perspective since in either case the bank receives full repayment of the debt. For this reason, the lender will carry out an audit every time the debtor declares CF_1, which will happen with probability α_1, with monitoring costs amounting to $\alpha_1 c$. The loan's interest rate is determined, as usual, by the following equation, with the only modification being that the lender's net income in the bad state 1 is reduced by the auditing costs:

$$(1 + r)L = (\alpha_2 + \alpha_3)(1 + r_L)L + \alpha_1(CF_1 - c)$$

$$(1 + r_L) = \frac{(1 + r)L - \alpha_1(CF_1 - c)}{(\alpha_2 + \alpha_3)L}$$

It is crucial to emphasize that the borrower's apparent information advantage can be self-defeating, because in the end it increases the cost of debt, once the expected monitoring costs are a component of the interest rate – the lender is determined to reach a *net* expected return equal to r. Also noteworthy is that both the dishonest and the honest borrower, who is always willing to announce the true cash flow, endure the interest rate increase.

Graphically, the problem takes the following form (figure 1.3).

From figure 1.3 we can establish the borrower's expected profit and the lender's and auditor's expected revenues (table 1.7).

The root of the problem is the borrower's temptation to declare a cash flow CF_1 that, even when true, the lender cannot verify without incurring monitoring costs. The common extra cost for all types of borrowers is the higher debt service, which jumps from $[(1 + r_L)L]_N$ to $[(1 + r_L)L]_{MC}$. By reading the first row in table 1.7, we find that under no monitoring, dishonesty pays off (the dishonest borrower earns $(C + G)$ more than the honest one) at the expense of the lender's expected income, but cheating stops being convenient under monitoring. As the lender threatens to audit, the dishonest borrower reviews his strategy – that is, monitoring aligns the incentives of both lender and borrower.[8]

---

[8] Actually, as far as the lender seizes enough cash flow to reduce the dishonest borrower's expected profit below $(A + E)$ – the honest borrower's profit – and not necessarily zero, the incentive compatibility is restored.

Table 1.7 *Expected profit and expected revenues*

	Without monitoring		With monitoring	
	Honest	Dishonest	Honest	Dishonest
$E\pi$	$A+B+E+F$	$A+B+E+F+C+G$	$A+E$	0
EI_{Lender}	$C+D+G+H+J$	$D+H+J$	$C+D+G+H+J$	$C+D+G+H+J+A+E$
$EI_{Auditor}$	0	0	$B+F$	$B+F$

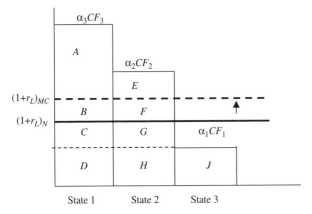

Figure 1.3 Distribution of EV under monitoring costs

A new aspect of the asymmetric information problem is the appearance of the auditor, who obtains the portion $(B + F)$ of the expected value of the project. Although it is the lender who carries out the control, the monitoring arising out of asymmetric information represents a social waste of resources that could end up in the hands of the entrepreneur.

1.3 Discussion

Is asymmetric information a relevant concept for understanding capital markets? We have argued here that in order for this to happen, uncertainty about the project outcome and a potential financial damage to the lender arising from his lack of information must be present. Both phenomena affect the majority of financial contracts. Every investment involves risk – moreover, competition between firms guarantees that there cannot be risk-free investment opportunities offering returns higher than the interest rate. At the same time, cases in which the lender is immunized from opportunist actions on the part of the borrower are rare. Thousands of bankruptcies every day are clear evidence that both the borrower's and lender's fortunes are intimately intertwined.

Having validated the existence and significance of the problem, let us briefly consider its dynamics. The borrower's incentive strategy rests on extracting an extra gain at the expense of an uninformed lender. But rational lenders are aware of their informational inferiority and cover themselves in different ways. In the final equilibrium, *it is the better-informed group (borrowers) that are supporting the costs of asymmetric information and, what is more unfortunate, low-risk and honest borrowers end up involuntarily providing a cross-subsidy to high-risk and dishonest borrowers.*

It is necessary to clarify that the sanctions are economic and not legal. In our analysis, the borrower who defaults does not face trial and her assets are not expropriated. The choice of a risky project in place of an agreed-upon conservative endeavour is a matter difficult to prove in a court, because it is always possible to attribute the eventual failure to a stroke of bad luck, since in the end all projects are to some extent risky. When dishonesty is in the form of misrepresenting revenues, and the lender can prove this through an audit, this can give rise to legal action. In fact, the adopted solution (seizing control of the effective revenues if deceit is verified) has an effect similar to an executive legal action that penalizes the lender who fails to fulfil his part of the contract.

Before finishing, the ethical aspect of financial contracts must be addressed. Our borrower is an individual who does takes the opportunity to fool the lender by hiding risk or profits. The economic and financial theory revolves around individuals whose sole objective is to maximize monetary gain, and thus have no morals. The undeniable existence of asymmetric information behaviour in the real world leads us sadly to admit that such representation is not just a theoretical simplification.

Bibliography

Akerlof, G. (1970), 'The market for lemons', *Quarterly Journal of Economics*, 84(3), 488–500.
   The first modern approach to the adverse selection problem.
Eatwell, J., M. Milgate and P. Newman (eds.) (1989), *Allocation, Information, and Markets, The New Palgrave*, London: Macmillan.
   A series of short articles about asymmetric information problems written by outstanding researchers in the field.
Ross, S. R. Westerfield and J. Jaffe (1996), *Corporate Finance*, 4th edn., New York: Irwin.
   An excellent textbook on corporate finance that covers some of the issues dealt with in this chapter.
Varian, H. (1992), *Microeconomic Analysis*, New York: W.W. Norton.
   An intermediate microeconomics book, chapter 25 focuses on the economics of information.

2　Protective mechanisms against asymmetric information

The borrower's information advantage can give him a benefit at the lender's expense. However, we have seen that the lender reacts rationally by making the associated costs borne by the borrower. For this to happen, we have realistically postulated that the lender can always invest his money in an alternative use providing him with the return he requires. In contrast, the borrower relies on external financing to undertake any project, and therefore must accept the conditions imposed by the lender. As a result, high-quality borrowers are charged an unfairly high interest rate.

In chapter 1 we limited ourselves to the major features of the asymmetric information analysis. In particular, we made two important simplifications. On the one hand, we allowed credit to flow from lenders to borrowers every time, omitting situations in which the lender interrupts this flow despite the existence of potential demand. In this chapter, we study the conditions under which voluntary credit rationing appears in response to asymmetric information.

On the other hand, we postulated that financially damaged borrowers passively accepted this situation. In practice, these borrowers try to send a signal about the actual quality of their projects with the purpose of avoiding the extra costs created by the lender's misinformation. Collateral, internal funds and covenants are frequently used signals. Likewise, financial contracts can be designed in ways other than debt to alleviate the consequences of information imperfections. Although these devices are to some degree helpful, both theory and reality agree that they are only partial remedies.

2.1　Credit rationing

We already know that, having all relevant information, the lender would charge a higher rate to the riskier projects. But in the context of asymmetric information the interest rate may become a perverse mechanism to discriminate bad from good risks, once the latter will be forced to pay an excessively high rate. Since the safer projects are particularly hit by the interest rate, they are the ones that will be turned away from the credit market in the first place in the event of an increase in interest rates that eliminates any profit for the entrepreneur. In principle, this is not a major obstacle for the lender, who has only to adjust the interest rate upward to reflect the rise in the overall risk of his loan portfolio. The serious drawback shows up whenever the surviving, riskier projects do not reach a positive profit threshold either at the new prevailing interest rate. In this case, the lender comes across the paradox that an interest rate rise *decreases* his expected income, inducing him to desist from raising the interest rate.

At this point, the positive effect of a higher rate (an increased income if the project succeeds) is outweighed by the negative effect (the attraction of projects with a low probability of repayment). Since at the new interest rate there will remain risky projects with an unsatisfied demand for credit, we are in the presence of **credit rationing**.

Credit rationing is far from being an efficient mechanism to solve our informational problems, but it is handy to limit the risk taken by the lender. We must emphasize the difference between the credit market and other markets for goods and services. As a general rule, in every market the price adjusts to equalize supply and demand; if demand is high, the price rises, the quantity supplied rises and an equilibrium is attained where demand equals supply. Nevertheless, in the credit market a higher demand for funds bids up the interest rate, but the supply of loanable funds might not respond, thus creating an excess of demand over supply which forces the rationing of the available funds.

We shall expand on the consequences of rationing using the chart in figure 2.1.

To interpret figure 2.1, let us recall how the lender sets the interest rate when there exists adverse selection:

$$(1 + r_L) = \frac{(1 + r)}{p_s}$$

where r_L is the loan interest rate, r is the lender's required return and p_s is the weighted probability of success. Let us now ask ourselves: what is going to happen if, for any reason, the expected return r rises? In a first approach, according to the last equation, the increase in r leads to a linear increase in r_L, which means that the lender's expected income will go up at the same pace.

However, the interest rate increase erodes the type A borrower's expected profit, so eventually we reach an interest rate at which this group leaves the credit market:

$$E\pi_a = EV_a - \alpha_{a,s}(1 + r_L)L = 0$$

$$(1 + r_L)|_{E\pi_a=0} = \frac{EV_a}{\alpha_{a,s}L}$$

In terms of figure 2.1, the initial upward tranche in the lower graph of figure 2.1 depicts the positive impact on the lender's expected income from an increase in r. But the negative effect, represented by the abrupt decline of EI, soon emerges, once the higher interest rate expels type A borrowers when their expected profit goes to zero, as shown in the upper graph of figure 2.1.[1] This change in the risk of the loan portfolio (now all borrowers are

---

[1] Recall that the lender charges $(1 + r_L) = (1 + r)/p_s$ whenever the pool of borrowers comprises both types of projects. Keeping the same interest rate, a fall in the probability of repayment from p_s to $\alpha_{b,s}$ implies that the lender is unable to reach its required return, and that is why it needs to raise the rate to $(1 + r_L) = (1 + r)/a_{b,s}$.

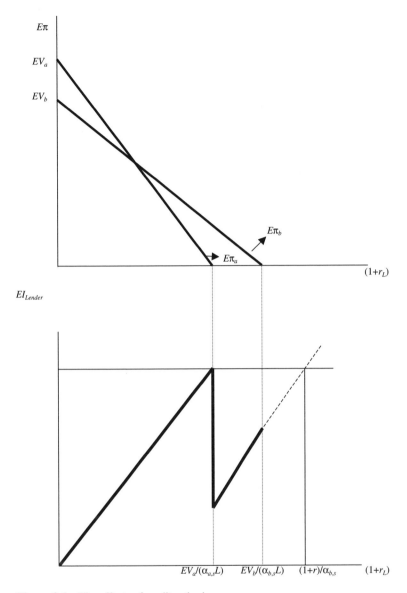

Figure 2.1 The effects of credit rationing
Note: We assume $EV_a > EV_b$ for reasons to be explained later.

type B) reflects itself in a reduction of the probability of success from p_s to $\alpha_{b,s}$ and the consequent higher interest rate:

$$(1 + r_L) = \frac{(1 + r)}{\alpha_{b,s}}$$

From here, it remains to find out if the new interest rate is affordable for type B borrowers such that they are still willing to apply for a loan. Credit rationing will prevail whenever the interest rate that makes it possible for the lender to lend exceeds the one beyond which no profit is accrued by the borrower:

$$\frac{EV_b}{\alpha_{b,s}L} < \frac{1+r}{\alpha_{b,s}} \quad \text{Or}$$

$$EV_b < (1+r)L$$

A project like this, whose expected value does not even cover the opportunity cost of the invested funds, is a **speculative project**. It would be undertaken using internal funds, because a bank deposit would be more profitable. However, in spite of being an unviable business from a productive standpoint, it might be attractive on financial grounds when funded by debt in a marketplace contaminated with adverse selection. Under these circumstances, the debt contract will be unsatisfactory to at least one of the parties: if the interest rate stays below $[(1 + r)/\alpha_{b,s}]$, there will be no supply of credit, while if above $[EV_b/\alpha_{b,s}L]$, there will be no demand. Since both participation constraints cannot be simultaneously met, the market for credit will vanish. Of course, as far as $EV_b > (1 + r)L$, this missing market situation will not materialize.

Let us highlight some points that deserve further attention. In the first place, note that increasing the lender's expected income, EI_{Lender}, is not the same as increasing his profits, which by the assumption of perfect competition are always zero. We are assuming here that r_L jumps as a consequence of a rise in r driven, for example, by a jump in the return on government bonds or in the international interest rate, which implies that the opportunity cost has risen.[2]

The next issue has to do with the lender's reaction in the face of the rise in r. We can prove right now with a numerical example that the lender will not charge an interest rate r_L higher than $[EV_a/(\alpha_{a,s} L)]$, and that he will rather choose not to lend (table 2.1).

We start by assuming $r = 10$ per cent, which means that the unique interest rate is $r_L = 120$ per cent (once again, the absolute lack of realism of this interest rate comes from the high risk of type B projects). Although both projects are profitable, it is suggestive that $E\pi_b > E\pi_a$ in spite of the fact that $EV_a > EV_b$. When $r = 25$ per cent, the interest rate climbs to 150 per cent and type A entrepreneurs reap no profit whatsoever. This rate is the one that eliminates all profit, $(1 + r_L) = [EV_a/(\alpha_{a,s} L)]$. Strikingly, at this rate project B still yields a positive profit. However, the lender knows that, with an interest rate slightly above 150 per cent, the information problem disappears (all borrowers are type B) and along with it the credit market collapses: type B projects, now lacking any asymmetric information shield, cannot resist the interest rate of 317 per cent $(1.25/0.3 = 4.17)$ – profit is already nil at 250 per cent $[105/(0.3 \times 100) = 3.5]$. The lender is certainly right in acting against his first impulse of raising the interest rate.

---

[2] Clearly the interest rate can also increase, for instance, if the lender perceives that the overall repayment risk has increased as a consequence of worse economic conditions. In terms of our equations, this means that p_s becomes lower.

Table 2.1 *The lender's reaction to a rise in r*

	Project A	Project B
CF_s	250	350
CF_f	0	0
α_s	0.7	0.3
α_f	0.3	0.7
EV	175	105
I	100	100
p	0.5	0.5
$r = 0.1$		
r_L	1.2	1.2
$E\pi$	21.0	39.0
EI	154.0	66.0
$r = 0.25$		
r_L	1.5	1.5
$E\pi$	0.0	30.0
EI	175.0	75.0

Let us also take a moment to understand why a speculative project not only survives in the market but also gets a higher benefit than a high-productivity, low-risk project. Two reasons explain this paradox: (a) in the bad event, the limited liability liberates the borrower from repayment; (b) in the good event, the profit is big because the interest rate is fixed, independent of the cash flow, and reduced by the existence of adverse selection.[3]

In table 2.2 we reproduce information presented by Petersen and Rajan (1994) on the financing of 3,404 small companies (fewer than 500 employees) in the United States.

Observing column (2), we can appreciate the potential existence of credit rationing: only 34 per cent of this sample of small businesses, those most likely to suffer information asymmetries, have access to some kind of debt. For the same reason, this percentage rises to 91 per cent for those of the largest size. The data also shows the severity of credit rationing even for those that already have debt, especially when we notice the importance of the debt provided by the owner or his relatives, an understandable situation given that in these cases information barriers are less significant. It is also clear that trade credit ('Other firms') is not a major source of funding, revealing that the presumed information advantage of suppliers does not seem to be confirmed by data. At the same time, the weight of bank debt is evident in all categories. We shall return to this point in chapter 6, where we shall discuss the information advantages of banks *vis-à-vis* other financial intermediaries.[4]

---

[3] Credit rationing can eventually emerge also in the context of moral hazard and monitoring costs as long as there are speculative projects seeking credit.

[4] We should make clear that the data suggest but do not prove the existence of credit rationing. It is possible, for instance, that other financing sources are cheaper and there is no need to use debt, in which case firms would not be facing any rationing. Alternatively, there would be a low demand for debt, and therefore it would not

Table 2.2 *Access to debt by small firms in the United States, based on 3,404 firms of fewer than 500 employees*

Size[a] (1)	% of firms with access to debt (2)	Fraction from each source					
		Bank (3)	Non-bank (4)	Owner (5)	Family (6)	Other firms (7)	**Total** (8)
1	0.34	55.4	10.9	14.1	15.2	4.3	**100.0**
2	0.55	61.5	13.2	12.1	9.9	3.3	**100.0**
3	0.71	63.0	12.0	9.8	12.0	3.3	**100.0**
4	0.82	61.1	12.2	12.2	10.0	4.4	**100.0**
5	0.91	66.7	13.3	11.1	5.6	3.3	**100.0**
6	0.91	68.9	15.6	7.8	3.3	4.4	**100.0**

Note: [a]Firms classified in six categories in descending order according to book asset value.
Source: Petersen and Rajan (1994).

2.2   Signalling

At this point we are fully aware that low-risk firms are adversely affected by the lack of information on the part of the lender. One way of alleviating this problem is the use of credible **signals** conveying the intrinsic soundness of the project, so as to avoid the premium lenders' charge to deal with adverse selection. A possible, but not very useful, device is the mere announcement that the project is sound and productive. As this strategy is costless, it can be employed by any borrower, regardless of the quality of its project. Trustworthy signals are those that bear an immediate cost to the borrower and whose reward is the access to lighter credit conditions. The point is strengthening the lender's confidence upon some limited liability to gain cheaper credit. *In order to be effective a signal should be costly to all borrowers, but more importantly it should be prohibitively costly to the riskier borrower.*[5]

Signalling is a partial solution to the problems posed by imperfect information. First of all, bad projects can manage to send the same signals as good ones, and still obtain positive profits. Besides, good projects without an adequate asset backing will continue to be confused with bad projects.

Collateral
Collateral is an asset of the borrower that is automatically transferred to the lender should the project revenues not be sufficient to repay the loan in full. In the context of adverse selection, the main party interested in offering this guarantee is the borrower with the most secure project, who bears a financing cost that is unjustly high. As the collateral reduces

---

be necessary to restrict its offer. Anyway, although a more rigorous analysis is certainly required to make a indisputable claim, figure 2.0 gives us a good reason to wonder.

[5] Although our approach will be mostly focused on the adverse selection problem, it must be said that signals are also helpful in the struggle with both moral hazard and monitoring costs. This should not be surprising, once we recognize that entrepreneurs are more unlikely to jeopardize their projects when they partially finance them with their own money.

the limited responsibility of the borrower in presence of an unfavourable result, a type A entrepreneur will be transmitting a signal concerning the quality of her project.

A borrower that offers a guarantee to cover part of the debt in the event of project failure is implicitly declaring the probability of success to be high. This decision involves a cost, given that she will lose the pledged assets if the project fails. However, type B entrepreneurs, aiming to be similar to type A ones, can do the same until a natural limit appears: the point at which the expected benefit fades away. The guarantee constitutes an effective signal when type B projects are excluded from capital markets, thus eliminating any problem linked to asymmetric information.

We can see what effect the collateral has on the expected benefit of the borrower. When both projects have the same expected value and both borrowers offer the same collateral C, the expected benefit of each project is given by:

$$E\pi_a = EV - (-1 + \alpha_{a,f})(1 + r_L)L - \alpha_{a,f}\,C$$
$$E\pi_b = EV - (-1 + \alpha_{b,f})(1 + r_L)L - \alpha_{b,f}\,C$$

where the interest rate is defined by:

$$(1 + r_L) = \frac{(1 + r)L - p_f C}{p_s L}$$

and p_s and p_f are the weighted probabilities of success and failure already introduced in chapter 1. The guarantee reduces the interest rate as it minimizes the lender's losses if the project fails. *We then have two conflicting effects: the higher cost of the loan when the result is unfavourable-represented by the guarantee – and the lower cost when the result is favourable-represented by the reduction in the interest rate.* By inserting the definition of the interest rate into the expected profit, we can check that the guarantee C reduces the expected profit for type B borrowers and increases it for type A borrowers:

$$E\pi_i = \alpha_{i,s}\left[CF_{i,s} - \frac{(1+r)L - p_f C}{p_s}\right] - \alpha_{i,f}C$$

$$= \alpha_{i,s}\left[CF_{i,s} - \frac{(1+r)L}{p_s}\right] + \left[\frac{\alpha_{i,s}}{p_s}p_f - \alpha_{i,f}\right]C$$

where $i = A \circ B$. Given that $p_f > \alpha_{a,f}$ and $\alpha_{a,s} > p_s$, posting collateral favours type A borrowers; in turn, as $p_f < \alpha_{b,f}$ and $\alpha_{b,s} < p_s$, the collateral diminishes the profit of type B borrowers. Intuitively, the reason is that the probability of losing the collateral is higher for the riskier borrower, preventing him exploiting his limited liability in the bad scenario. Graphically, the situation would look like that in figure 2.2.

At collateral level C^*, where the incentive to undertake type B projects vanishes, the only surviving projects are those of type A and thus the new interest rate falls to reflect their lower risk. The vertical jump in A's profit is explained by the interest rate adjustment from $[(1 + r)/p_s]$ to $[(1 + r)/\alpha_{a,s}]$, until reaching the non-asymmetric information level,

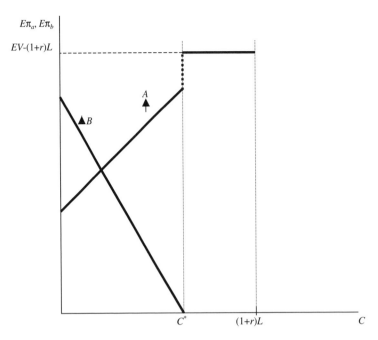

Figure 2.2   Collateral as an effective signal

$[EV - (1 + r)L]$.[6] Once again, note that the main beneficiary of the lower repayment risk is not the lender but the borrower.

Let us now examine the effect of collateral when all borrowers are type A:

$$E\pi_a = \alpha_{a,s}[CF_{a,s} - (1 + r_L)L] - \alpha_{a,f}C$$

$$= \alpha_{a,s}\left[CF_{a,s} - \frac{(1 + r)L - \alpha_{a,f}C}{\alpha_{a,s}}\right] - \alpha_{a,f}C$$

$$= \alpha_{a,s}\left[CF_{a,s} - \frac{(1 + r)L}{\alpha_{a,s}}\right]$$

$$= EV - (1 + r)L$$

As far as asymmetric information is no longer a relevant issue, collateral has no impact on the borrower's profit either. The gain in terms of interest rate in the good event is exactly compensated by the loss in the bad event. As shown by the last equation, the entrepreneur obtains a fair return: the project's expected value less the income required by the lender, thus satisfying both parties.

---

[6] The horizontal axis finishes at $(1 + r)L$ because a collateral higher than the amount of debt would be redundant – with such collateral the debt is risk-free and the interest rate is equal to r, with or without asymmetric information. However, in the real world, the collateral is frequently larger than the debt. This occurs because lenders correctly anticipate that the price of the assets serving as collateral may be volatile and that it takes considerable time and money to collect them.

The contrast between the case in which both project types coexist under adverse selection and the latter case without asymmetric information leads us to an important conclusion: *the widespread use of collateral is an undeniable indicator of the practical relevance of asymmetric information in financial markets.*

Evidence supports this assertion. We present some data gathered by Booth and Chua (1995), who studied a sample of 1,347 high-amount loans in the United States, with an average value of US $184 million, finding that 45 per cent of them were guaranteed. Another paper by Berger and Udell, cited by Booth and Chua, shows that 70 per cent of a large sample of loans, smaller than US $50,000, were covered with collateral. Note here that the size of the loans does not alter the general conclusion: small and large borrowers are exposed to information problems.

Before going on, a note of caution is in order. As the reader has surely noticed, collateral is effective if two conditions are met: (i) Type A entrepreneurs have enough assets to post as much collateral as C^*. If not, entrepreneurs with safe projects but no assets may not be able to reveal their true type; and (ii) There actually exists a level of collateral $C^* < (1 + r)L$. As can be seen in figure 2.2, if the type B profit function is flatter, this will not always be the case, implying that the signal is not effective.[7]

Internal funds

The use of internal funds is another signal that trustworthy borrowers can resort to in order to distinguish themselves. As with collateral, by tying his fortune to that of the project, the borrower is expressing his confidence in the project and voluntarily giving up his limited responsibility in the case of a negative result. Denoting internal funds as IF and the type of borrower as i ($i = A$ or B), the borrower's expected profit becomes:

$$E\pi_i = \alpha_{i,s}[CF_{i,s} - (1 + r_L)L] - (1 + r)IF$$
$$= \alpha_{i,s}[CF_{i,s} - (1 + r_L)(I - IF)] - (1 + r)IF$$

It can be observed that the internal funds carry an *opportunity cost* to the entrepreneur: by investing his own money on the project, he loses the return he would obtain by making an alternative financial investiment, say, a bank deposit. With the usual definition of the interest rate, the last formula can be stated as follows:

$$E\pi_i = \alpha_{i,s}\left[CF_{i,s} - \frac{(1 + r)}{p_s}(I - IF)\right] - (1 + r)IF$$

$$= \alpha_{i,s}\left[CF_{i,s} - \frac{(1 + r)}{p_s}I\right] + \left[\frac{\alpha_{i,s}}{p_s} - 1\right](1 + r)IF$$

As project A's probability of success is higher than the weighted probability of success of both projects, $\alpha_{a,s} > p_s$, internal funding raises the profitability of this type of project, while

---

[7] Another drawback of collateral is that it is likely to diminish the incentives to gather information on the borrower. For incipient entrepreneurs with highly productive projects, this constitutes a serious obstacle for growth. Conversely, entrepreneurs with sufficient assets will easily obtain credit, no matter the intrinsic quality of their projects. Certainly, the allocation of credit will not be optimal.

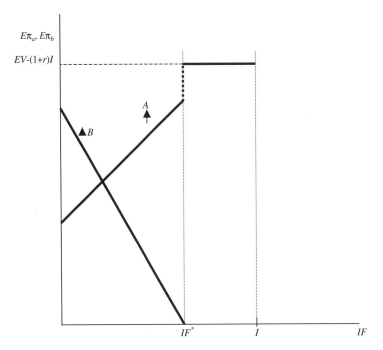

Figure 2.3 Internal funds as an effective signal

the opposite happens with type B projects. We can translate all this information to a graph (figure 2.3).

Having reached IF^*, the type A borrowers manage to distinguish themselves from type B borrowers, who exit the credit market.[8] Also notice that from IF^* on and until the project is fully self-financed ($I = IF$), the expected profit of the type A entrepreneur remains at its maximum level, regardless of how the portion ($I - IF^*$) is financed. From here, as in the absence of asymmetric information $\alpha_{a,s}$ and p_s are equal, we can deduce that:

$$E\pi_a = EV - (1+r)I$$

As neither IF nor L appear in the formula, we can assert that the firm's profit is independent of the source of funding. As seen in chapter 3, this is a fundamental principle of corporate finance.

To provide some evidence on the role of internal funds in mitigating information problems, the data in table 2.3, extracted from Japelli and Pagano (1994), display for sixteen OECD countries the maximum mortgage loan as a share of the total property value, the rest being the required amount of owner's internal funds (down payment).

It can be observed from table 2.3 that in no country do banks lend 100 per cent of the property value, with ratios fluctuating between a minimum of 50 per cent (Turkey and Greece) and a maximum of 95 per cent (Denmark).

---

[8] As a final remark, bear in mind that the effectiveness of this signal is threatened by the same factors discussed at the end of the previous section on collateral.

Table 2.3 *Maximum ratio loan/property value (per cent)*

Country	Value[a]	Country	Value[a]	Country	Value[a]
Germany	80	Finland	85	Norway	80
Australia	80	France	80	New Zealand	80
Austria	60	Great Britain	87	Netherlands	75
Belgium	75	Greece	50	Portugal	60
Canada	80	Ireland	90	Sweden	95
Denmark	95	Italy	56	Turkey	50
United States	89	Japan	60		
Spain	80	Luxembourg	60		

Note: [a] Average values for 1981–7.
Source: Japelli and Pagano (1994).

Contractual clauses

The credit agreement generally includes a series of clauses that protect the rights of the lender. The acceptance of these clauses is a positive signal to the bank and can result in a smaller interest rate for the borrower. There are **negative clauses**, which inhibit certain actions by the company, and **positive clauses**, in which the firm is obliged to take certain measures. Negative clauses include restrictions over dividend distribution, the transfer of assets and the issue of additional debt without prior authorization from the bank. Positive clauses include, among others, a minimum level of required working capital and the periodic provision of financial reports.

The practice of agreeing upon clauses is standard in the real world. Ross, Westerfield and Jaffe (1996) cite evidence revealing that 91 per cent of public debt issues in the United States include the prohibition of issuing additional debt, 39 per cent of realizing mergers and 36 per cent of selling shares.

As in other cases, these covenants do not completely rectify the absence of adequate information. Their main weakness is that the bank is prevented from observing and controlling the firm. Although the company agrees to certain rules, it enjoys ample discretion in its operation. If discovered, it may suffer penalties that result in bankruptcy, but it is not easy for the lender to verify the violation nor to prove it in court – the lender has no direct control on the use of the funds and cannot convincingly assert whether the default is due to a switch toward riskier projects or just a stroke of bad luck.

2.3   Issue of shares as an alternative source of funding

Up to this point, our analysis has been centred on debt (loans or bonds) as the sole source of funding, omitting the existence of other alternative sources such as the issuance of **shares**. The two main features of this financial contract are that the obligation is contingent on the project's outcome (not fixed as in a debt contract) and that the risk sharing is with the **shareholder**. Before going into detail, let us see the operation of a share contract. The first step is to determine the **market price**, P – that is, the value that the shareholders would be willing to pay if they are to obtain their required return r. As any rate of return r is the ratio between expected income and cost, in this case, the expected value EV over the price P:

$$1 + r = \frac{EV}{P}$$

$$P = \frac{EV}{1 + r}$$

Once valued over the whole project, the entrepreneur will sell in the market just a fraction, I/P, so as to fund the initial investment I, and will keep the remaining shares as compensation for his managerial work.

How does the problem of adverse selection affect the relationship between the borrower and lender in this context? Surprisingly, there is absolutely no effect. To see why, we will compare the compensation between the borrower and lender with financing by shares and debt. With debt, we have already seen that:

$$E\pi = EV - \alpha_s(1 + r_L)L$$

$$EI_{Lender} = \alpha_s(1 + r_L)L$$

while with shares:

$$E\pi = \left[1 - \frac{I}{P}\right]EV$$

$$EI_{Shareholder} = \left[\frac{I}{P}\right]EV$$

Unlike the debt contract, now not only the borrower's profit but also the shareholder's income depends upon the expected value EV. Accordingly, *as we assume that the share-holder does know the expected value common to projects A and B, the lack of information becomes irrelevant*. The shareholder correctly appraises both projects because he needs to know only EV, without worrying about the project's probability of success (note that α_s does not appear either in $E\pi$ or in EI above). In the debt contract, given the initially fixed interest rate, an erroneous estimation of the actual probability of success reduces the lender's expected income. On the contrary, under a share contract, the shareholder's income is independent of this probability: although he may have believed that he was dealing with a type A project (high probability of success) when it was actually a type B one (low probability), his revenue will not be undermined because this low probability is counterbalanced by a high cash flow.

Table 2.4 *Debt and share contracts:*
a numerical example

	Project A	Project B
CF_s	300	700
CF_f	0	0
α_s	0.7	0.3
α_f	0.3	0.7
EV	210	210
I	100	100
r	0.1	0.1

In sum, *under the above conditions, the share contract is immune to adverse selection and moral hazard.*[9] In a world free of asymmetric information and equal expected value for all the projects, the debt and share contracts would be equivalent, except for the fact that revenues would be more variable in the latter case. Let us use the same numerical example seen in the treatment of adverse selection in chapter 1 to fix these concepts (table 2.4).

The reader can corroborate that, in both cases, the project's market value is $190.9 ($210/1.1 = 190.9$), and that the shareholder will grab the 52.4 per cent of the expected value ($100/190.9 = 0.524$). The entrepreneur's expected profit will be $100 ($0.476*210 = 100$). Since this profit is the same for both projects, the entrepreneur has no temptation to cheat about the actual project undertaken, which guarantees by itself that asymmetric information is not an issue here. In other words, this contract is incentive-compatible. Since the shareholder simply gets the rest of the expected value, she will receive $110 no matter what project is being financed.[10]

To visualize the difference between debt and equity, let us take a look at figure 2.4, where we represent on the horizontal axis a large number of possible expected cash flows in ascending order.

To the left of Default cash flow, the lender takes the entire cash flow $CF < (1 + r_L)L$, while to the right he receives $(1 + r_L)L$. In turn, the shareholder gets a share $0 < (I/P) < 1$ of each possible cash flow. The total area $(a + b + c + d + e + f)$ is the expected value of the project. The bank's expected income is $(a + d + b + e)$. The area $(d + e + c)$ represents the shareholder's expected income. Given that the shareholder and the lender require the same expected income, $(1 + r)I$, it follows that:

$$EI_{Lender} = EI_{Shareholder}$$
$$(a + b + c + d + e) = (d + e + c)$$

---

[9] Does this contract solve the monitoring problem? Not necessarily, since the entrepreneur will choose the project with the higher cash flow in good events, since his profit from hiding the real cash flow will be greater.

[10] Notice that these calculations are based on expected values, the only piece of information available at the moment of writing the contract. But when the project matures, the shareholder will receive either $156 (project A) or $364 (project B). Again, this does not mean that he will be better off by choosing project B, because the probability of success is very small.

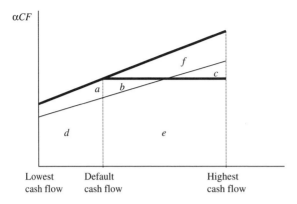

Figure 2.4 The difference between debt and equity

And, since the expected value is also the same, the entrepreneur reaps the same expected profit under either contract:

$$E\pi(Debt) = E\pi(Shares)$$
$$(f + c) = (a + b + f)$$

From figure 2.4 it is apparent that the shareholder's income is much more volatile than the lender's: when things go well, the shareholder obtains a very high income but, being a business partner, he gets a modest return in an ugly event.[11]

We should not think that the issue of shares is a cure for the complications caused by asymmetric information. In fact, shares are the least employed source of funding, and several issues, once again linked to information problems, justify the reluctance of many companies to issue these securities. On the one hand, if the potential shareholders have problems distinguishing between projects with different expected values, the best projects will suffer the already well-known consequences of adverse selection. (In chapter 3 we shall pay attention to the adverse selection problems in the stock market.) On the other hand, it is clear that the announcement of false revenues continues to be relevant when investments are financed through shares. As seen in the following section, the shareholder needs to spend more resources to monitor a share than a debt contract.

2.4 Monitoring costs under share financing

Let us go back to the case examined in section 1.2 on monitoring costs. Under share financing, the market price of the project comes from:

$$P = \frac{\alpha_1 CF_1 + \alpha_2 CF_2 + \alpha_3 CF_3}{1+r} = \frac{EV}{1+r}$$

---

[11] Note that the risk we are referring to here should be understood as variability across possible events, and not the repayment risk, which is the most relevant concept of risk to us. In fact, the shareholder faces no repayment risk, in the sense that he is now owed a fixed amount of money. Finally, we will see in chapter 8 that volatility is relevant when investors are risk averse.

With an initial investment I, the entrepreneur will get an expected profit $E\pi = (1 - I/P)EV$, and in each of the three possible events his profit will be:

$$
\left[
\begin{array}{c}
\left[1 - \dfrac{I}{P}\right]CF_1 \\[2ex]
\left[1 - \dfrac{I}{P}\right]CF_2 \\[2ex]
\left[1 - \dfrac{I}{P}\right]CF_3
\end{array}
\right\}
\text{when the realized cash flow is}
\left\{
\begin{array}{c}
CF_1 \\[2ex]
CF_2 \\[2ex]
CF_3
\end{array}
\right.
$$

Since the share $(1 - I/P)$ is predetermined, the entrepreneur will be tempted to declare a cash flow lower than that actually generated by the project. Aware of this, the shareholder will decide to audit the firm whenever the entrepreneur announces CF_1 and CF_2 (since the shareholder knows that CF_3 is the maximum cash flow attainable, there is no need to verify it). Following the previous argument, the new market valuation will be:

$$
P = \frac{EV - (\alpha_1 + \alpha_2)c}{1 + r}
$$

The price fall due to the costly verification of revenues reduces the entrepreneur's share in the expected value. In comparison with the debt contract, it is noticeable that the expected monitoring cost is lower in the latter case [$\alpha_1 c$ against $(\alpha_1 + \alpha_2)c$]. Bearing in mind that it is the entrepreneur who finally pays for these costs, he will prefer the contract that minimizes such costs, that is, the debt contract. Based on this insight, we can understand why the debt contract is a much more popular financing instrument than the simpler sharing of gains and losses.[12]

2.5   Alternative financing instruments

In a traditional debt or equity offering, the investor needs to assess the overall ability of the firm to generate enough cash flow to pay for the required return. An ingenious way to minimize the associated information problems is to link the ability to repay to a subset of assets which, in one way or another, can produce the necessary cash flow with a high degree of certainty and regardless of the performance of the firm as a whole or the behaviour of

---

[12] Maturity and liquidity are two additional features that distinguish the debt from the share contract. Debt represents a fixed nominal obligation with a certain **maturity**, while equity has neither of those features. In particular, the fact that equity financing is not redeemable makes it especially well suited to finance long-term projects. Besides, shares can be traded in stock exchanges, permitting investors with appetite for **liquidity** to transfer their holdings to other investors on the spot – of course, this will work fine as far as markets are deep and competitive. However, we must say that some loans can become liquid through securitization (see the next section).

its managers. This is the financial engineering behind such instruments as securitization, leasing and factoring.

In a **securitization** transaction, the firm isolates some assets with predictable revenues, for example trade receivables, by selling them to an independent entity, known as *special purpose vehicle*, thus effectively separating the risk of the company from that of the assets themselves. In turn the special purpose vehicle issues securities which, as a result of the better credit quality of the backing assets compared to that of the firm as a whole, carry a lower interest rate than normal debt. Furthermore, there exist *credit enhancement* techniques to raise the credit quality of the securities issued, such as the segmentation between senior tranches (which have first claim on assets and cash flows in case of default) and subordinated tranches (which absorb the resulting losses); the constitution of a reserve account to cover some losses; and the purchase of a financial guarantee insurance.

Strictly speaking, asset securitization is not credit in that, instead of supplying funds today to finance an asset that will produce cash flows to repay that credit in the future, it only liquefies existing assets. But nevertheless securitization delivers several potential benefits, as the firm can use the proceeds to acquire assets with a higher earning power, to increase liquidity, or to retire expensive debt, among other uses. Because of these benefits, securitization has grown at an impressive pace since the 1980s; as an example, in the United States issues went from a modest US$ 4 billion in 1985 to US$ 360 billion in 1998.

In a **leasing** contract, the firm (the lessee) is allowed to use an asset owned by the other party (the lessor), who retains the legal ownership of the asset and receives periodic payments for its services. Security for the transaction is provided by the asset itself, which can be repossessed by the lessor if the lessee fails to meet a payment. The lessee typically has the right to buy the asset at the end of the contract for a nominal fee. Compared to a regular collateralized transaction, the distinctive feature of leasing is that the same asset simultaneously serves as collateral and additional cash flow-generating capital equipment. Also, because the assets legally belong to the lessor, repossession is less costly than with a normal guarantee. In all, leasing improves the access and costs of financing, especially for firms with no credit history or collateral. This financing mechanism has evolved significantly since the 1960s, with more than US$315 billion of leases written in developed countries, representing 15 per cent of private investment (US$140 billion in the United States, where leasing penetration reaches only 30 per cent). In developing countries, a less intense use of leasing is observed, but the trend is quite steep, as demonstrated by the fact that it went up to 11 per cent of private investment in 1994 from only 4 per cent in 1988.

Yet another instrument is **factoring**, which simply consists in the discount of trade receivables issued by low-risk clients with banks or a specialized intermediary. Once again, the risk faced by the buyer of the invoice is not that of the selling firm but that of its low-risk client. Although credit obtained by this means is most often short term, the possibility of getting rid of the usual information problems markedly reduces financing costs.

Having presented their specific benefits, it must be said that these markets are expanding but are still only mildly developed compared to traditional debt and equity contracts, particularly in developing countries. The principal reason is that the correct functioning of these markets relies upon an efficient legal and enforcement setup ensuring that creditors are repaid under the terms agreed upon. After all, this *legal risk* can in practice be as important as *credit risk* at the time of assessing repayment risk. We will devote part of chapter 5 to discussing this legal dimension of financial markets.

2.6   Other deterrent mechanisms

While the problems described so far are certainly present in everyday financial transactions, one must argue that many entrepreneurs do not behave opportunistically despite the serious difficulties lenders have in detecting such actions.[13] It is a good time to introduce some real-world dissuasive factors counterbalancing asymmetric information that come not from the contract design or the control exerted by the lender and the shareholder but from the incentives of the entrepreneur. These factors appear once we recognize that firms do not run just one project and that its assets are totally consumed over the life of such a project, as implied in our analytical setup. Actual firms have long-term planning horizons, implying that **reputation** comes into play. Bankruptcy is costly not only for its direct costs (as seen in chapter 3) but also for its reputational costs. The manager of a financially distressed firm intending to take on new projects will find it extremely expensive or even impossible to obtain financing, not to mention the question mark hanging over his professional and personal prestige.[14]

Reputation is also crucial to ensure a fluid access to outside financing for growing firms. Issuers of stock that may want to go back to the market on a regular basis to fund new projects in the future will try to keep the interest of investors in buying new issues by paying reasonable dividends and providing transparent and reliable information on the firm's performance. This *reputation-building* behaviour is perhaps more valuable when dealing with a bank, because loans are typically short term, which means that the bank can threaten the firm with the cancellation of its credit line if the loans are not serviced when due or if a hidden action is detected.

Additionally, the liquidation of the firm may cause the firm to suffer the accelerated depreciation of some assets. That will be the case when the firm possesses specific assets lacking a secondary market to resell them at market prices or, even worse, if it has intangible assets such as goodwill or trademarks.

All in all, the one-time gain from dishonesty will pay off only when it outweighs this set of costs.

2.7   Discussion

We are now ready to draw a number of lessons about the operation of financial markets. Investors are not naive and react positively when faced with the possibility of being fooled. In chapter 1 we looked at the functioning of financial markets under the assumption that, even

---

[13] Clearly, we cannot claim that every default case is due to the choice of risky over conservative projects. Default can result from the very riskiness of any project and from unexpected adverse shocks on the firm.

[14] Bankruptcy laws and public registers make it difficult for entrepreneurs to liquidate a firm and initiate a new one leaving past defaults behind. (On this subject, see chapter 5.)

with inefficiencies, the supply and demand of capital are in equilibrium. In this chapter we moved toward the possibility that information frictions would be so severe that they would discourage either lenders or borrowers from participating in the market, and, even worse, exclude low-risk projects in the first place.

Likewise, we have revised the assumption that the owners of safer projects passively accept the damage indirectly inflicted by the owners of risky projects. In practice, as the lender places the responsibility on the borrower, the entrepreneur has an opportunity to send a signal concerning his project's quality. Collateral and internal funds fit into this category. The general conclusion is that none of these devices completely solves the information problem, but they do lessen some of the consequences.

Another interesting finding is that debt markets give rise to an inefficient allocation of credit. On the one hand, the safest projects are unfairly punished with too high an interest rate as a consequence of informational problems. Share contracts are better suited for this purpose, but new information problems inhibit the development of the primary stock exchange market.

As a closing note, let us point out that, in spite of the significant role played by asymmetric information, many entrepreneurs are likely to behave honestly just in response to their own, selfish goals, without needing external control from lenders or the government. This is because default in several respects deters the entrepreneur, who will face both reputational and pecuniary costs. In short, dishonesty delivers short-term gains that must be compared to long-term costs.

Bibliography

Booth, J. and L. Chua (1995), 'Structure and pricing of large bank loans', *Economic Review, Federal Reserve Bank of San Francisco*, 3, 52–62.
  A micro-level analysis of bank lending policy in the United States.
Fazzari, S., G. Hubbard and B. Petersen (1988), 'Financing constraints and corporate investment', *Brookings Papers on Economic Activity*, 1, 141–95.
  In the first part of the book there is an explanation of the role of internal funds in business investment.
Hillier, B. (1997), *The Economics of Asymmetric Information*, New York: St Martin's Press.
  A recommendable book that explains the implications of information problems in different contexts – capital markets, labour, health and insurance.
Japelli, T. and M. Pagano (1994), 'Saving, growth and liquidity constraints', *Quarterly Journal of Economics*, 109, 83–109.
Petersen, M. and R. Rajan (1994), 'The benefits of lending relationships: evidence from small business data', *Journal of Finance*, 49, 3–37.
  Detailed information of the structure of small-firm financing in the United States.
Romer, D. (1996), *Advanced Macroeconomics*, New York: McGraw-Hill. Chapter 8 discusses in detail the origin and consequences of monitoring costs on business investment.
Ross, S., R. Westerfield and J. Jaffe (1996), *Corporate Finance*, 4th edn., New York: Irwin.
  Cited in chapter 1.
Stiglitz, J. and A. Weiss (1981), 'Credit rationing in markets with imperfect information', *American Economic Review*, 71, 393–410.
  An original theoretical article expounding on credit rationing and the importance of guarantees.

Part II Applications to corporate finance

3 Asymmetric information and corporate financing

It is hard to refute the idea that the value of a firm depends on the quality of its investments and not on how they are financed. Indeed, if the cost of financing or capital cost is the same for all sources of funds, then financial factors will be irrelevant. This is the governing principle of corporate finance, elaborated by Franco Modigliani and Merton Miller in 1958. However, this theorem, which we shall discuss in section 3.2, is valid only if capital markets are perfect, in the sense that they are free of information problems, intermediation costs and taxes. In the real world, this perfection does not exist, a fact that leads us to challenging and enriching extensions.

In general terms, the value of a firm will be at a maximum when the best projects are selected and the cost of capital is minimized. Among the different flaws of the credit market, we shall focus our attention on asymmetric information. In the presence of asymmetric information, not only the cost of capital but also the criteria for selecting projects will change with the financing structure of the firm. By weighing costs and benefits, the company will try to find the **optimal financing structure**, one that maximizes the company's value given its productive resources. In the Discussion section (p. 59) we will summarize the different pros and cons at the time of choosing the debt to equity ratio.

Informational flaws are relevant in this context because they cause conflicts of interest between the different stakeholders of the firm, in which the better informed ones can take advantage at the expense of others, even when by doing this the value of the firm as a whole shrinks. On the one hand, as a natural extension from chapters 1 and 2, shareholders tend to choose the options that raise their own profits, lowering those of the lender. On the other hand, as a new aspect to be developed in this chapter, we shall face the conflicting relation between the shareholders and the manager of the firm.

So far, we have studied the firm as a whole unit. Abandoning simplicity for reality, we must admit that in modern societies we usually observe that property and management are in many ways separated. Whether it is the case that the property is dispersed in a large number of shareholders or that shareholders prefer to delegate the daily management to specialized staff, many firms are conducted by their managers. Managers are hired and remunerated in order to maximize the stockholders' interests. Unfortunately, the relationship between manager and stockholders is not free from tensions, originating in the imperfect correlation between the gains generated by the manager and his remuneration. In the extreme case that the manager has a fixed income, he will not be overly concerned about net profits, as long as they cover his own pay. Under these circumstances, it is possible for the manager to carry out hidden actions which increase his own profits while reducing those of the stockholders, who lack the necessary flow of information and power to control him. This particular information problem is the so-called **agency** or **principal–agent** problem, because it identifies the frictions between the owner, or principal, and a delegate, or agent. We shall develop this topic in the following section.

These information conflicts end up affecting the cost of capital as well as the quality of productive investment. The first lesson we have learned from chapters 1 and 2 is that external financing, the financing that comes from debt or shares issued in financial markets, is infected by information problems. Consequently, internal funds are cheaper than external funds. The existence of a pecking order in the financing sources is developed in section 3.3. The composition of the liabilities side between debt and capital not only affects risk preference but also the amount of investment and the effort and efficiency in the management of the firm. We shall examine these effects in detail throughout this chapter.

We would not have a complete picture of the corporate financing decision process if we did not pay special attention to the role of taxes imposed upon firms, stockholders and lenders. Although beyond the scope of asymmetric information, taxes represent an exaction of profits that the firm will try to minimize by choosing carefully between debt and capital, as each of them is subject to different tax procedures. Similarly, the legal and administrative costs of liquidating a bankrupt firm are paid by the firm, which will try to minimize them. As the probability of bankruptcy increases with more debt, these costs are one of the factors that influence financing policy.

Before deepening the analysis of these issues, let us take a look at the real world to see how capital structure varies in different countries.

3.1   How are companies financed in the world?

A recurrent theme in specialized articles is the outstanding growth in the volume and sophistication of financial markets since the 1970s. For example, between 1965 and 1995 the size of the banking system (measured as the ratio between credit to the private sector and gross domestic product, GDP) has grown from 57 per cent to 100 per cent in Germany, from 81 per cent to 118 per cent in Japan, from 11 per cent to 61 per cent in Korea and from 24 per cent to 149 per cent in Taiwan. Stock markets have experienced similar growth. The number and speed of transactions and the variety of available instruments have surpassed any optimistic forecast. The trading volume in derivative instruments (options, futures and swaps) has multiplied more than ten times since 1990. In the United States alone, 220 million transactions involving credit take place daily, with a volume of US\$ 1.6 billion (a higher value than the whole annual production of Latin America).

However, financial statements of non-financial firms – those not devoted to financial intermediation, such as banks and other institutional investors – reveal a very different

Table 3.1 *Total debt to assets ratio around the world,*
non-financial, listed firms[a]

Country	Total debt/Assets
Developed countries	
United States	0.27
Japan	0.35
Germany	0.16
France	0.25
Italy	0.27
United Kingdom	0.18
Canada	0.32
Latin America	
Argentina	0.24
Brazil	0.17
Chile	0.24
Mexico	0.29
Peru	0.15
Venezuela	0.23

Note: [a]The data correspond to 1991 for developed countries
(*Source*: Rajan and Zingales, 1995) and the average 1992–6
for Latin America (*Source:* calculated from Economatica,
www.economatica.com).

reality: *asset accumulation is financed mainly with internal funds*.[1] In the first place, take a look at the total debt to assets ratio, with debt including short- and long-term bank credit and bonds. In table 3.1 we can see this ratio for public firms in selected developed and Latin American countries.

As can be seen, this ratio is low in both developed countries and Latin America, in all cases apart from Japan below 35 per cent. One should bear in mind that we are talking about public firms, which have better access to external funding than privately owned businesses. Strikingly, in spite of their disparate financial deepening, there seems to be no significant difference between the two groups of countries.

We may obtain a better measure of the preference for retained earnings by looking at how the *flow*, rather than the stock, of assets is financed. This procedure has many advantages. The first is that accounting standards differ across countries, and in general balance sheet information has many flaws, sometimes involuntary (valuation problems) and at other times deliberate (tax reasons). In contrast, the sources and uses of cash flows can be more precisely measured than balance sheet items, which reflect historical, rather than current, financial and investment decisions. In table 3.2 and 3.3 we show aggregate information about sources of funds in developed countries and Latin America.

---

[1] In the discussion section at the end of the chapter we offer some basic elements of corporate accounting, the main source of empirical studies on corporate finance. Readers with previous knowledge of fundamental accountancy principles may skip this explanation.

Table 3.2 *Sources of funds in non-financial firms in developed countries, 1990–1995, as a percentage of total sources*

Country	Debt	Shares	Retained earnings	**Total**
Austria	−2.7	9.6	93.1	**100.0**
Canada	31.0	11.8	57.1	**100.0**
Italy	24.9	9.1	66.0	**100.0**
Japan	41.6	5.2	53.2	**100.0**
Holland	17.1	17.6	65.3	**100.0**
Sweden	20.5	−1.0	80.4	**100.0**
Spain	26.9	11.4	61.7	**100.0**
United States	−7.9	15.6	92.2	**100.0**
Average	**18.9**	**9.9**	**71.1**	**100.0**

Source: Calculated by the author from OECD, *Financial Statistics*, various years.

Table 3.3 *Sources of funds in non-financial firms in Latin America, 1990–1996, as a percentage of total sources*

Country	External debt	Issues of shares	Internal bonds	Internal bank credit	Retained earnings	**Total**
Argentina	4.1	3.7	6.4	6.9	79.0	**100.0**
Brazil	5.7	2.6	5.5	10.1	76.1	**100.0**
Chile	11.2	5.6	14.2	9.0	60.2	**100.0**
Colombia	2.2	1.9	4.0	12.4	79.6	**100.0**
Mexico	3.0	3.3	4.6	4.4	84.7	**100.0**
Peru	1.4	0.3	2.2	8.4	87.8	**100.0**
Venezuela	−4.5	0.4	4.4	0.8	96.8	**100.0**
Average	**3.3**	**2.5**	**5.9**	**7.4**	**80.6**	**100.0**

Source: Bebczuk (1999).

The figures in tables 3.2 and 3.3 strengthen our previous conclusion about the dependence of the firms on retained earnings. Two consistent features are evident in both groups:

(1) The *prevalence of retained earnings*, which contribute an average of 71 per cent of total sources in developed countries and 81 per cent in Latin America. However, the ratio is not uniform across countries;
(2) The *predominance of debt over stock* in the external sources of the firms, and within the debt, of bank credit over negotiable bonds. In Latin America, domestic bank credit represents 7.4 per cent of total sources, followed by domestic bonds (5.9 per cent), international debt (3.3 per cent) and stock issues (2.5 per cent). Looking closely at the figures for developed countries, the same pattern emerges, with debt participation at 18.9 per cent and shares at 9.9 per cent.

This pattern challenges the intuition that derives from the extraordinary growth of financial markets. However, the theory of imperfect information, our driving idea, brings us a clear and convincing explanation. The numerous credit operations that take place daily in modern economies are of a very short-term nature and include items ranging from check issues, payments with credit and debit cards and the purchase and sale of financial instruments and their derivatives. In these cases, the creditor is virtually risk-free: in most of those financial transactions, the debtor is required to have a margin or collateral, whereas with credit and debit cards the seller can easily find out whether the debtor has enough funds or has not exceeded his credit limit. This level of certainty is not conceivable in longer-term credit relations involving productive decisions. When a firm enters capital markets, information problems are inevitable.

3.2   The Modigliani–Miller Theorem

The modern theory of corporate finance began in 1958 with an article by Franco Modigliani and Merton Miller in which a challenging proposition was put forward: *if capital markets work perfectly, the capital structure of a firm is irrelevant*.[2] A company's value depends upon the profitability of its assets and not on the way in which such investments are financed. The **Modigliani–Miller Theorem** is the basis for the rest of this chapter and most of the following ones, which explains the attention we shall focus upon it in this section.

The main idea is that, given a certain productive project, an entrepreneur cannot raise his expected benefit $E\pi$ by simply changing the mix between internal funds, debt and shares. Similarly, we shall show that the existence of repayment risk does not alter this result. The project in question has the following expected value:

$$EV = \alpha_s CF_s + \alpha_f CF_f$$

The initial investment is I, which can be financed with internal funds IF or with a loan of L:

$$I = IF + L$$

Let us begin with the case where the debt is safe for the lender regardless of the project's outcome, which requires that:

$$CF_s > CF_f > (1+r)L$$

---

[2] Modigliani and Miller's original demonstration of their theorem was different from the one we use here. Supposing that a perfect capital market exists, with investors who can lend and borrow at the prevailing interest rate, two companies that generate the same cash flows should have the same market value. If, for example, an indebted company has a higher market value than a firm without debt, investors of the debt-free firm can gain by taking on debt themselves to acquire the indebted company until replicating by means of home-made leverage the financial structure of the first, and making a risk-free profit. Since this kind of arbitrage is infeasible in a competitive financial market, both firms should have the same value at all times. The idea was so revolutionary and incisive that Modigliani and Miller received the Nobel Prize in Economics in 1986 and 1990, respectively, in part for this discovery.

In this case, the interest rate will be exactly the same as the required rate of return, $r_L = r$, and the entrepreneur's expected profit will be:

$$
\begin{aligned}
E\pi &= \alpha_s[CF_s - (1+r)(I - IF)] + \alpha_f[CF_f - (1+r)(I - IF)] - (1+r)IF \\
&= (\alpha_s CF_s + \alpha_f CF_f) - (\alpha_s + \alpha_f)(1+r)I + (\alpha_s + \alpha_f)(1+r)IF - (1+r)IF \\
&= EV - (1+r)I
\end{aligned}
$$

where we use the fact that $L = I - IF$, the opportunity cost of internal funds is r and $\alpha_s + \alpha_f = 1$. The last expression demonstrates the irrelevance of capital structure, as neither IF nor L appear in the last formula, meaning that only the intrinsic quality of the productive project, and not the way in which it is financed, determines the entrepreneur's profit. The underlying intuition is that the lender seeks on his funds the same yield that the entrepreneur does, r, in which case the origin of I lacks any importance. Thus, given r, the only way to increase earnings is to select projects with the highest possible expected value and the lowest possible I.

It is in general the case that a certain degree of uncertainty surrounds the ability to repay the debt, creating a wedge between the required yield and the interest rate on the loan. With risky debt, the interest rate is determined by the following equation:

$$(1+r)L = \alpha_s(1+r_L)L + \alpha_f CF_f$$

The lender appropriates all income in the unfavourable event (under which the income is not enough to repay the debt), while in the case of success, he is repaid the debt plus the following interest rate:

$$
\begin{aligned}
(1+r_L) &= \frac{(1+r)L - \alpha_f CF_f}{\alpha_s L} \\
E\pi &= \alpha_s[CF_s - (1+r_L)(I - IF)] - (1+r)IF \\
&= \alpha_s\left[CF_s - \left[\frac{(1+r)(I - IF) - \alpha_f CF_f}{\alpha_s(I - IF)}\right](I - IF)\right] - (1+r)IF \\
&= (\alpha_s CF_s + \alpha_f CF_f) - (1+r)(I - IF) - (1+r)IF \\
&= EV - (1+r)I
\end{aligned}
$$

Clearly, the previous result still holds. Does the situation change, if, instead of debt, the external financing consists of shares? From chapter 2, we know that if the market price of the project is $P = EV/(1+r)$ and the external financing is $(I - IF)$, external shareholders will reap a fraction $[(I - IF)/P]$ of the expected value, with which the entrepreneur's expected profit is:

$$
\begin{aligned}
E\pi &= \left[1 - \frac{I - IF}{P}\right]EV - (1+r)IF \\
&= \left[1 - \frac{(1+r)(I - IF)}{EV}\right]EV - (1+r)IF \\
&= EV - (1+r)I
\end{aligned}
$$

In conclusion, in a perfect world free of asymmetric information, transaction costs and taxes, the entrepreneur should worry about finding the best opportunities of productive investment, since the cost of capital is the same regardless of where the funds come from. Financing decisions do not create wealth by themselves. In what follows we will challenge this claim when capital markets suffer from imperfections.

3.3   Adverse selection and the pecking order of financing sources

As we already saw, a company can finance the acquisition of new assets by using:

(1) Internal funds
(2) Debt
(3) Stock issues.

We have just observed that this is precisely the order of preference that companies reveal in practice.[3] With astonishing precision, our asymmetric information framework will lead us to that theoretical prediction. To demonstrate this, we shall rely on our introduction to adverse selection in chapter 1. Just as before, the lender's unsolvable dilemma is to determine if the project in search of financing is type A or B. Trusting the entrepreneur to tell the truth would be futile, since type B entrepreneurs have clear incentives to disguise the project as A, which ruins the credibility of true type A entrepreneurs.

A substantial difference is that now we shall suppose that the expected value of projects A and B are not the same but rather $EV_a > EV_b$, with $\alpha_{a,s} > \alpha_{b,s}$. The cash flows in the event of success and failure are CF_s and CF_f, respectively, and they are identical for both projects, but this assumption is not essential. Also, and this is crucial, $CF_s > (1 + r)L > CF_f$, implying that the projects are not immune to bankruptcy. The expected value of the two projects is then given by:

$$EV_a = \alpha_{a,s}CF_s + \alpha_{a,s}CF_f$$
$$EV_b = \alpha_{b,s}CF_s + \alpha_{b,s}CF_f$$

We shall now compare the cost of financing under the different sources. Let us begin with the case of shares. In the absence of asymmetric information, the market price of each project is:

$$P_a = \frac{EV_a}{1+r} = \frac{\alpha_{a,s}CF_s + \alpha_{a,f}CF_f}{1+r}$$
$$P_b = \frac{EV_b}{1+r} = \frac{\alpha_{b,s}CF_s + \alpha_{b,f}CF_f}{1+r}$$

Once project A offers higher expected cash flows, its valuation is necessarily higher than that of project B. However, unable to distinguish between both projects, the market will

---

[3] Let us make clear that 'pecking order' refers to the financing of additional investment, not to the firm's capital structure, i.e. the composition of the liabilities' side of the balance sheet. The debt / to capital ratio will be an important concept in the following sections.

determine a common value for both:

$$P = \frac{p_a EV_a + p_b EV_b}{1+r}$$

$$P = \frac{p_s CF_s + p_f CF_f}{1+r} = \frac{EV}{1+r}$$

where p_a and p_b represent, as before, the proportion of projects A and B in the economy. Given adverse selection, if there are a large number of projects, p_a and p_b can be taken as the probabilities of choosing a project of each type at random. Since EV is an average of the expected values of projects A and B, it can be seen that:

$$P_a > P > P_b$$

This inequality means that the market undervalues the most profitable project and over-values the least profitable one. If we keep in mind that the entrepreneur's share depends directly on the external shareholders' valuation, it is apparent that adverse selection discourages the issuance of shares for the best projects and encourages it for the worst ones, as reflected in the expected profit function for each entrepreneur type:

$$E\pi_a(Shares) = \left[1 - \frac{1}{P}\right] EV_a$$

$$E\pi_b(Shares) = \left[1 - \frac{1}{P}\right] EV_b$$

Paying attention to debt financing, we already know that in absence of asymmetric information the interest rate is determined from the following equations:

$$(1+r)L = \alpha_{a,s}(1+r_{L,a})L + \alpha_{a,f}CF_f$$

$$(1+r)L = \alpha_{b,s}(1+r_{L,b})L + \alpha_{b,f}CF_f$$

from which the corresponding interest rates are:

$$(1+r_{L,a}) = \frac{(1+r)L - \alpha_{a,f}CF_f}{\alpha_{a,s}L}$$

$$(1+r_{L,b}) = \frac{(1+r)L - \alpha_{b,f}CF_f}{\alpha_{b,s}L}$$

If we attach to each group probabilities p_a and p_b, in the presence of adverse selection there will be a unique interest rate r_L:

$$(1+r_L) = \frac{(1+r)L - p_f CF_f}{p_s L}$$

As we have seen before, this lender behaviour implies that:

$$r_b > r > r_a$$

which implies that the expected profit for each type is:

$$E\pi_a(Debt) = EV_a - \alpha_{a,s}(1+r_L)L - \alpha_{a,f}CF_f$$
$$E\pi_b(Debt) = EV_b - \alpha_{b,s}(1+r_L)L - \alpha_{b,f}CF_f$$

The entrepreneur's decision on whether share or debt financing is more convenient boils down to whether the following expressions are positive or negative:[4]

$$E\pi_a(Shares) - E\pi_a(Debt) = (1+r)L\left[\frac{\alpha_{a,s}}{p_s} - \frac{EV_a}{EV}\right] + CF_f\left[\alpha_{a,f} - \frac{\alpha_{a,s}p_f}{p_s}\right] < 0$$

$$E\pi_a(Shares) - E\pi_a(Debt) = (1+r)L\left[\frac{\alpha_{a,s}}{p_s} - \frac{EV_a}{EV}\right] + CF_f\left[\alpha_{a,f} - \frac{\alpha_{a,s}p_f}{p_s}\right] < 0$$

Type A projects need to be financed by debt, while type B projects are financed through shares. Without being too rigorous, we can identify the first term of the right-hand side of each equation as an **'undervaluation effect'** and the second as a **'limited liability effect'**. The undervaluation effect reflects the penalty that the market applies on good projects $(P_a > P)$ and the undeserved reward on bad ones $(P_b < P)$. The limited liability effect, on the other hand, identifies the expected loss in a bad event under a debt contract, which is bigger for type B projects $(\alpha_{b,f}CF_f > \alpha_{a,f}CF_f)$, that is, the limited liability becomes smaller.[5] The combined incidence of both effects reinforces B's preference and A's reluctance concerning the share contract.

It is possible to separate analytically the undervaluation effect from the limited liability effect by assuming that the debt is safe $(\alpha_{a,f} = \alpha_{b,f} = 0)$:

$$EV_a(Shares) - EV_a(Debt) = \left[1 - \frac{I}{P}\right]EV_a - [EV_a - (1+r)I]$$

$$EV_b(Shares) - EV_b(Debt) = \left[1 - \frac{I}{P}\right]EV_b - [EV_b - (1+r)I]$$

Recalling that $P = EV/(1+r)$, we derive the following expressions:

$$EV_a(Shares) - EV_a(Debt) = (1+r)I\left[1 - \frac{EV_a}{EV}\right]$$

$$EV_b(Shares) - EV_b(Debt) = (1+r)I\left[1 - \frac{EV_b}{EV}\right]$$

Here we have isolated the effect attributable to the unfair stock market valuation. Under adverse selection, we know that $EV_a > EV > EV_b$ and therefore the pecking order is still at work.[6] However, the most interesting point is that, without asymmetric information,

---

[4] To sign the expressions, we use our assumptions on the values of the intervening variables, as in previous cases. A numerical example checking these results can be found later in this section (p. 46).
[5] Notice that assuming that $CF_f > 0$ is essentially the same as having posted collateral. In the same vein, note that, for the same CF_f, the lower the probability of success, the less attractive a debt contract is for type B borrowers. This would not happen if CF_f were zero, since in such a case there is full limited liability.
[6] With safe debt, asymmetric information is no longer an issue, so neither project can reap an abnormal benefit from the borrowing option.

Table 3.4a *Choosing how to finance an investment project*

	Project *A*	Project *B*
CF_s	200	200
CF_f	100	100
α_s	0.7	0.3
α_f	0.3	0.7
EV	170	130
I	100	100
r	0.1	0.1
p	0.5	0.5
Debt		
Without adverse selection		
r_L	0.14	0.33
$E\pi$	60.0	20.0
EI_{Lender}	110.0	110.0
With adverse selection		
r_L	0.20	0.20
$E\pi$	56.0	24.0
EI_{Lender}	114.0	106.0
Shares		
Without adverse selection		
P	154.5	118.2
$E\pi$	60.0	20.0
$EI_{Shareholder}$	110.0	110.0
With adverse selection		
P	136.4	136.4
$E\pi$	45.3	34.7
$EI_{Shareholder}$	124.7	95.3

$EV = EV_a$ for project A and $EV = EV_b$ for project B, so that the two equations equal zero. Accordingly, the expected profit would be equal to that attainable under self-financing:

$$E\pi_a = EV_a - (1+r)I$$
$$E\pi_b = EV_b - (1+r)I$$

In conclusion, in order to minimize the cost of capital, good entrepreneurs choose their sources of funding according to the following pecking order: first, internal funds; when these are exhausted, safe debt, then risky debt, and, as a last resort, stock.[7] The numeric example in table 3.4 captures the essence of the previous discussion.

[7] Although safe debt has the same cost as internal funds, this will not be true when intermediation costs exist, as they do in capital markets. Actually, even ignoring asymmetric information, we would have a 'pecking order' based on transaction costs, since internal funds are free from such costs, and equity issues are quite expensive compared to debt (especially bank loans).

Table 3.4b *Equity issue as a bad signal*

	Project A	Project B
P	118.2	118.2
$E\pi$	26.2	20.0
$E I_{Shareholder}$	143.8	110.0

Table 3.5 *Cost of capital: 1*

	Project A	Project B
Internal funds (%)	10.0	10.0
Debt (%)	14.0	6.0
Stock (%)	24.7	−4.7

It is clear that the best projects will make their financing decisions based on the pecking order, with the bad ones acting in the opposite way – for instance, the type B entrepreneur barely returns $95.30 of the $100 collected through the equity issue, which means that the effective cost of capital is negative![8]

However, this convincing story is incomplete. Bear in mind that the market knows the characteristics of each project, but it cannot distinguish among them owing to its information shortcomings. But the chosen source of financing conveys a valuable (and free-of-charge) signal to the market: in particular, the announcement of a stock issue reveals that the entrepreneur is type B, since type A will prefer to apply for debt instead. Once type A entrepreneurs announce their intention of applying for debt, type B's opportunistic behaviour will be exposed – once his true type is known, the cost of capital in stock markets will increase from −4.7 per cent to 10 per cent (the cost under no asymmetric information). And if a type A dares to issue shares, he will be judged as a type B and will suffer a pronounced undervaluation.[9] This twist alters the distribution of the project's expected value in the following way (table 3.4b).

Table 3.5 allows us to calculate the effective cost of capital under adverse selection, measured as the ratio between the financier's expected income and the initial investment I.[10]

In terms of the cost of capital, table 3.6 can be read as in table 3.5.

Ironically, the market's rational reaction undermines the profitability of the most valuable projects – as no trustworthy signal is available on the actual quality of the project, the

---

[8] The attentive eye will note that the financier always obtains his required return of 10 per cent with any alternative source: $0.5 \times 0.10 + 0.5 \times 0.10 = 0.5 \times 0.14 + 0.5 \times 0.06 = 0.5 \times 0.247 + 0.5 \times (-0.047) = 0.10$. Lenders and shareholders, aware of the eventual loss from type B borrowers, apply higher rates on type A entrepreneurs in order to reach the goal of 10 per cent.

[9] Type B will still find attractive a debt contract over self-financing, since in this case adverse selection still affects that contract.

[10] Note that the cost of financing is neither the expected yield r (both would coincide if repayment were certain) nor in the case of debt is the interest rate r_L (which is applied in favourable outcomes, but does not take into account the lender's income in an unfavourable outcome).

Table 3.6 *Cost of capital: 2*

	Project A	Project B
Internal funds (%)	10.0	10.0
Debt (%)	14.0	6.0
Shares (%)	43.8	10.0

market will rely on the information conveyed by the firm's actual decisions. An even more unfortunate consequence of adverse selection is that, once the capacity to obtain debt is exhausted, highly profitable projects may be passed up if they do not reach the following profit threshold:[11]

$$E\pi_a = \left[1 - \frac{I}{P}\right] EV_a = 0$$

$$\frac{I}{P} = 1 \text{ or } EV = (1+r)I$$

Predictably, the expected profit of both types of projects vanishes when the participation of outside shareholders is 100 per cent, i.e. when the market price of the project equals the initial investment. Keeping in mind that the market considers all projects to be type B, the market price will be given by $P = EV_b/(1+r)$ and the profit will be nil when $I \geq P$, or:

$$EV_b \leq (1+r)I$$

From this, we can deduce that type A projects, in spite of being highly profitable, will not be undertaken if they compete for funds with purely speculative projects. In other words, when resorting to external financing, *it is not only the quality of the project that is important but also the average quality of the pool of projects seeking funds.*

Many empirical studies have successfully documented the practical implications of this theory. The first piece of evidence at hand is our initial table 3.1 on actual financing decisions around the world. A second, and equally convincing proof, is that researchers have found that the market value of companies drops when they announce a stock issue, but that this does not occur when debt is issued.

Companies launching their **initial public offering (IPO)** of shares have an additional obstacle. In this case, the conflict does not focus on the entrepreneur and the shareholders as a whole, but rather among the potential shareholder groups that have different information with regard to the issuing company. As the potential investors' lack of information is more severe for those companies that have not previously issued shares, the stock price will be even lower. The root of the conflict is that there are informed investors who know the real value of the firm, and misinformed investors who are aware only of the expected value. Since the informed investors will buy only when the stock price is lower than the actual value, they will leave a smaller fraction of the offering for those misinformed, who, on the contrary, will bid and obtain all the issued stock when the market price is higher than the

---

[11] This argument parallels that of credit rationing in chapter 2.

true value. This way, misinformed investors buy more shares when it is unwise to do so. This phenomenon is called the '*winner's curse*'. However, the misinformed investors are not naive and know that they are in an unfavourable position. To make their stock attractive to this group of investors, the companies sell the shares below their expected value. Several studies have found that the stock price increases on average between 10 per cent and 35 per cent on the first day of offering, a gain that attempts to compensate the misinformed investors.

3.4 Financial structure and moral hazard

The debt to capital ratio of a firm tends to create pervasive conflicts of interest between shareholders and lenders of the firm. Two types of moral hazard behaviour may take place: risk preference or asset substitution, and underinvestment or debt overhang.

Risk preference refers to the bias toward risky projects whenever the firm is already highly indebted. Suppose that the company has an unpaid debt of L from a previous project.[12] However, before declaring itself bankrupt, it may choose to take on a new project from two options. To simplify, let us now suppose that the new project, with an initial investment I, is financed with internal funds that have a required return r. The expected value of these projects is given by:

$$EV_a = \alpha_{a,s} CF_{a,s} + \alpha_{a,f} CF_{a,f}$$
$$EV_b = \alpha_{b,s} CF_{b,s} + \alpha_{b,f} CF_{b,f}$$

with $\alpha_{a,s} > \alpha_{b,s}$, $\alpha_{a,s} CF_{a,s} > \alpha_{b,s} CF_{b,s}$ and $\alpha_{a,f} CF_{a,f} > \alpha_{b,f} CF_{b,f}$, implying that project A is more profitable and safer than B. At the same time, $CF_{a,f} < L$ and $CF_{b,f} < L$: with an unfavourable outcome, the income is not enough to repay the debt. Let us examine how much the old lender should expect to collect from the cash flow of the new project:

$$EI_{Lender} = \alpha_{a,s} L + \alpha_{a,f} CF_{a,f}$$

if project A is selected, or:

$$EI_{Lender} = \alpha_{b,s} L + \alpha_{b,f} CF_{b,f}$$

in the case of project B. It is easy to see that the lender would prefer the borrower to take on project A, but such a decision is made by the shareholders who run the firm. Recalling that the borrower will receive the residual expected value, the decision between the two projects will take into account the expected profit under each possible project:

$$E\pi_a = \alpha_{a,s}(CF_{a,s} - L) - (1 + r)I$$
$$E\pi_b = \alpha_{b,s}(CF_{b,s} - L) - (1 + r)I$$

The difference between them is:

$$E\pi_a - E\pi_b = (\alpha_{a,s} CF_{a,s} - \alpha_{b,s} CF_{b,s}) + (\alpha_{b,s} - \alpha_{a,s})L$$

---

[12] This is a big departure from our usual framework, in which the firm runs just one project and debt is required to finance such project. Here we introduce a more realistic approach, by allowing the firm to have debt accumulated from the past and to use cash flows from a new project to repay it.

Table 3.7 *Distribution of EV: 1*

	Project A	Project B
$E\pi$	2	6
EI_{Lender} (previous debt)	58	24
Funding of the new project	110	110
EV	170	140

There are two forces in conflict here: on one hand, the expected value and, on the other hand, the risk of the new projects. It should not be surprising that if ($\alpha_{a,s} CF_{a,s} > \alpha_{b,s} CF_{b,s}$), project A becomes a good opportunity because it increases the owner's residual right. But curiously, the larger its probability of success, the less attractive it is for the same owner! The reason is that if the new project is low-risk, the principal beneficiary is the lender, and his probability of repayment increases. This moral hazard dilemma is more subtle than other hidden actions, once it is concerned not with the project financed by the lender but rather with a future project. However, the conflict remains the same: the borrowers, favouring their own interests, make decisions that adversely affect the interests of the lender. Let us demonstrate this with a numerical example:

$$EV_a = 0.8 \times \$200 + 0.2 \times \$50 = \$170$$
$$EV_b = 0.4 \times \$350 + 0.6 \times \$0 = \$140$$

Both projects require an initial investment of $100. The unpaid debt (including interest) is $60. Project A's profit relative to B's is given by:

$$E\pi_a - E\pi_b = (\$160 - \$140) + (0.4 - 0.8) \times \$60 = -\$4$$

By comparing the situation under each of the mutually exclusive projects we find the situation in table 3.7.

Despite the higher expected value of project A, the indebted entrepreneur is inclined towards the less productive project B as a device to reduce the income appropriated by the lender. As shown in table 3.8, under project A the lender's expected income is $58 (0.8 × 60 + 0.2 × 50 = 58), but falls to $24 with project B (0.4 × 60 + 0.6 × 0 = 24).

This negative result is crucially dependent upon the borrower not being able to exercise or not exercising his limited liability, which in turn depends upon the relationship between CF_f and L. What if $CF_{a,f} = CF_{b,f} = \$60$? Let us see:

$$EV_a = 0.8 \times \$200 + 0.2 \times \$60 = \$172$$
$$EV_b = 0.4 \times \$350 + 0.6 \times \$60 = \$176$$

In this case $EV_b > EV_a$. Will the borrower choose the now less profitable project A? Table 3.8 shows otherwise.

Table 3.8 *Distribution of EV: 2*

	Project A	Project B
$E\pi$	2	6
EI_{Lender} (previous debt)	60	60
Funding of the new project	110	110
EV	172	176

Figure 3.1 Timespan of the investment project

As the debt is now secure – the lender is repaid in full in any scenario – whatever may be the chosen project, the borrower cannot take advantage of the defenceless lender. This re-establishes the compatibility of incentives between both parties. The borrower will find that the only manner of increasing his earnings consists in choosing the project with the higher expected value (note that now $E\pi_b - E\pi_a = EV_b - EV_a = 4$, suggesting that the entrepreneur's profit entirely relies on the intrinsic quality of the new project).

A related behaviour that is also provoked by the existence of previous debt is **under-investment** or **debt overhang**. The peculiar feature here is that the firm's dilemma now revolves around the decision whether to invest or not invest, rather than choosing between riskier and safer projects. We will see how the presence of previous debt can discourage a company from taking on highly profitable projects, since the lender will capture the profits. Let us consider project A, which is entirely financed by debt and has the following expected value:

$$EV_a = \alpha_{a,s} CF_{a,s}$$

yielding an expected profit of:

$$E\pi_a = \alpha_{a,s}[CF_{a,s} - (1 + r_L)L]$$

Now suppose that a new investment opportunity B becomes available and will mature together with the previous project (figure 3.1).

The new project constitutes an excellent opportunity, profitable and completely secure:

$$EV_b = CF_b > (1 + r)I$$

Should it be accepted, project B is financed by shares or by internal funds with an expected return r. From the entrepreneur's standpoint, the advantage of this project is its high profitability, and the disadvantage that its revenues may end up in the hands of the lender that financed project A. Project B will be clearly attractive if it could be financially independent from project A, but under an adverse scenario for this project, the lender has rights on the cash flows generated by project B. The decision will be based on the comparison between project A's expected profit and that of the combined project $A + B$:

$$E\pi_{a+b} = \alpha_{a,s}[CF_{a,s} + CF_b - (1 + r_L)L] - (1 + r)I$$

The most important part of this formula is that which does not appear in it, namely, the company's income being in an unfavourable state, in which case the company should receive $[CF_b - (1 + r)I]$, but this amount is appropriated by the lenders that financed the failed project A.[13] The difference between the two alternatives is:

$$E\pi_{a+b} - E\pi_a = \alpha_{a,s}CF_b - (1 + r)I$$

The negative incentive will vanish when the new project becomes very profitable (high CF_b), since the company can service the previous debt and still make some profit. The same holds true when the initial project A has low risk (high $\alpha_{a,s}$), which will liberate the new project from its inherited obligations. Otherwise, project B will not be undertaken in spite of its high profitability. We can check this result through a numerical example. Projects A and B have these characteristics:

$$EV_a = 0.7 \times \$200 = \$140$$
$$EV_b = \$150$$

The required rate is 10 per cent and the corresponding interest rate on project A is 57.1 per cent $[1.1/0.7 = 1.571]$. Both projects demand an initial investment of \$100. Expected profit in each case is:

$$E\pi_a = 0.7 \times [\$200 - \$157.1] = \$30$$
$$E\pi_{a+b} = 0.7 \times [200 + 150 - 157.1] - 1.1 \times \$100 = \$25$$

Clearly in this case the company will not proceed with project B once project A is already in operation. The addition of project B generates an expected loss of \$5 (\$25 − \$30 = −\$5): under the favourable state, in which project A's debt is covered by its own cash flows, the entrepreneur makes a net expected gain for project B of \$28 $[0.7 \times (\$150 - \$110) = \$28]$, but under the unfavourable scenario, the \$150 is partially used to cancel the unpaid debt of project A, \$157.1, generating an expected loss of \$33 $[0.3 \times \$110 = \$33]$ equal to the unrecoverable cost of funding the new project.

3.5 Management and property: the principal–agent conflict

The asymmetric information problems created by the separation of property and management have been ignored up to this point by assuming that the owner and the manager of the firm are the same person. But this is not a good description of the structure of many big firms, where a manager is hired to run the business on behalf of the shareholders. The delegation embodies a positive aspect in the sense that the daily command of the company

---

[13] The entrepreneur will not receive anything in the unfavourable scenario, unless $[CF_b - (1 + r)I] > (1 + r_L)L$, a situation that we will rule out as it is quite unrealistic.

lies with a competent professional, but it comes at a cost: a great deal of power lies in the hands of a party whose interests may be distinct from those of the shareholders, who may be unable to collect the information and exert the necessary control.

Beyond his power within the company, the manager is a mere employee of the owners of the company. The manager may be held responsible for bad outcomes, but he does not completely share the good ones because he does not possess 100 per cent of the capital. Consequently, his individual goals are not always aligned with those of the employer. What makes this incentive problem more acute is that, contrary to other labour contracts, the manager has very wide discretion and control over the funds and decisions of the company. Why cannot shareholders properly control the manager of their own company? The answer lies, first, in the fact that an employee's effort is not totally observable and, second, that the shareholders do not have the knowledge or time to closely monitor all decisions made by the manager (otherwise there would be no reason to hire a manager).[14] Moreover, as with other asymmetric information problems, the uncertainty surrounding all projects allows us to blame bad outcomes on bad luck instead of managerial negligence. These are the main features of the **principal–agent problem** between the shareholders (the principal) and their agent (the manager).

We will analyse two possible managerial actions that could affect the value of the company. The first deals with a lower-than-expected amount of managerial effort and the second with the preference for low productivity projects from the shareholders' standpoint but a high return from the manager's position.

Sometimes, the manager's opportunism takes the form of low effort. The source of the conflict with shareholders lies in the fact that the company's performance tends to improve with the manager's dedication to assess ongoing and new investment opportunities or closely to monitor the daily activity of the employees. A more concentrated managerial effort should translate into larger company earnings but not necessarily a larger managerial salary. A larger effort has related costs, such as the loss of managerial well being in terms of less leisure time and increased job-related stress (taking work home, staying in the office until midnight, or spending weekends at meetings). With a fixed salary, independent of the company's performance, the strategy to minimize the work effort (choosing to play golf in the mornings and leave the office early in the afternoons) can be a rational choice from the manager's perspective. The most direct method of personally involving the manager is by tying her rewards to the company's earnings, measured as the cash flows net of interest and taxes. A numerical example will help us elucidate how the effort's incentives depend on the manager's participation in the earnings. Let us suppose that the company's profits vary with the quantity of the manager's working hours as in table 3.9.

If the manager has a fixed income, say $10, it is clear that it is more convenient to work just 6 hours a day and spend the rest of the day in leisure. Let us see how the situation changes when the manager possesses company stock. If the manager possesses 10 per cent

---

[14] Clearly we are referring to the effort placed on activities where ability or intellect come into play. In contrast, it is easier to control activities that are more physically intensive, especially those based on a pre-established routine.

Table 3.9 *Managerial effort and company profits*

Working hours (per day)	Company profits ($)
6	100
10	120

Table 3.10 *Effort and manager's compensation (10% of company stocks)*

Working hours (per day)	Managerial compensation ($)
6	10
10	12

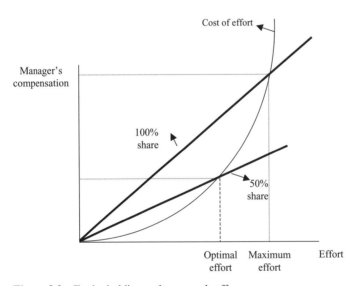

Figure 3.2   Equity holding and manager's effort

of the capital and does not have any fixed remuneration, her income will change with the earnings in the way shown in table 3.10.

   Profit sharing clearly encourages the manager to work 10 hours per day, simultaneously increasing the shareholders' gain and his own, thus making their initially disparate goals compatible.[15] The graph in figure 3.2 illustrates the point.

---

[15] We are assuming that the increase in compensation neutralizes the cost (or, technically speaking, the decreasing utility) of working more hours.

Table 3.11 *Manager's compensation and profit*

Manager's decision	Company profits	Manager's compensation	
		10% of the capital	30% of the capital
Buy the private jet ($)	80	18	34
Replace the machine ($)	120	12	36

In figure 3.2 we assume that the effort imposes a growing cost on the manager, who will expend effort such that marginal cost equals marginal benefit (if the marginal benefit exceeds the cost, it suits the manager to apply effort; if the cost exceeds the benefit, he will suffer a net loss). The manager will deliver the maximum effort (and corresponding cash flows) upon obtaining 100 per cent of the earnings – the proprietor–manager case that we have looked at up to this point.[16] When the manager's participation is less than 100 per cent, the effort is reduced for the simple reason that the manager does not gain in full for each dollar that he generated.

We now move to the case in which the manager chooses low-productivity projects. In accordance with the shareholders' directions, the manager's investment policy is governed by a very simple concept: choose all the projects that offer positive net value. The manager will be tempted to stray from this rule by applying funds to uses that increase her own well-being or personal power inside the corporation, maximizing the corporate wealth before that of the shareholders. By 'corporate wealth', we mean all investments over which the manager has obligations and direct management. These include personal perquisites, new and more luxurious offices and the acquisition of new firms. These investments increase the manager's power but do not necessarily increase the company's productive potential.

Let us evaluate the manager's behaviour when, in a somewhat exaggerated case, she has the alternative to buy a private jet for personal use or to replace an obsolete machine. The cost of both projects is $10, which the company possesses in cash. If she purchases the jet and keeps the old machine, the earnings of the company will decrease to $80, but the $10 cost of the jet is actually a payment to the manager. The manager's stock participation is crucial in the decision. Let us compare the present 10 per cent with an alternative of 30 per cent. The manager makes a table (table 3.11) (but does not show it at shareholders' meetings!)

With a 10 per cent share, the manager's personal compensation is bigger when buying the jet ($0.10 \times \$80 + \$10 = \$18$) than when replacing the machine ($0.10 \times \$120 = \$12$), but the situation is reversed when the share increases to 30 per cent ($34 versus $36). The change must be attributed to the fact that in this case the manager's remuneration is more closely linked to the earnings of the company, so she has an increased incentive to avoid an abrupt fall. In dealing with compatibility of incentives, we can prove that in this example

---

[16] The earnings participation of the manager and proprietor are respectively denominated inside equity and outside equity.

the shareholders benefit as well, noting that their earnings go from \$62 (\$80 − \$18 = \$62) if the participation is 10 per cent to \$84 (\$120 − \$36 = \$84) if the participation increases to 30 per cent.

We consider again the discussion concerning the company value and its financial structure. We have already seen what effect the managerial participation has on the company performance, but equally important is the fact that *the debt can positively influence the manager's behaviour, thus acting as a disciplinary device*. In the first place, we note that the purchase of the jet is possible because the manager uses available funds with no clear-cut alternative uses at hand or **free cash flows**. Debt represents an irrevocable compromise that limits the discretion of the manager to the highest degree, preventing her embarking on unproductive ventures. For example, suppose that the firm has \$100 free cash flows, which the manager may choose to apply to a project with an initial investment of \$100 and an expected value of \$105. The required return is as usual 10 per cent. Under these circumstances, it is in the shareholders' interests to decide (in the shareholders' meeting) a dividend payment of \$100. This way, shareholders will be able to obtain a return of 10 per cent on any financial assets rather than a modest 5 per cent by reinvesting in the firm. Besides, the need to raise debt with a cost of 10 per cent (or higher) will force the manager to select projects with a high expected value to avoid losing money for herself and the shareholders as a whole.

Secondly, if the manager's remuneration is part of the remaining funds, once the debt is repaid it will be in the common interest of the shareholders and the manager to increase the earnings instead of private interests. Thus, given a certain payment to the manager, the larger the company debt, the larger the manager's participation in the residual profit.[17] We have seen that the larger participation contributes to align the incentives of the shareholders and the manager.

It can be claimed that the previous example is unrealistic, once the board of directors has enough power to limit to some extent the manager's prerogatives and remove dishonest managers if necessary. Also, some managers' self-control will be exerted as an adverse company performance will damage her professional reputation, especially if it leads to default – furthermore, the probability of getting an equivalent job in another company after such an unbecoming exit is ostensibly lower. The threat of a **takeover** by another company affects the manager's effort as well, as a tender offer is itself a signal about a poor manager's job. We shall talk more about *agency* problems when dealing with corporate governance in chapter 5.

3.6 A digression: bankruptcy costs, taxes and financing structure

Although bankruptcy costs and taxes do not have a direct relationship with asymmetric information, they form part of the possible explanation for the choice of capital structure of the company and cannot be ignored if one desires a comprehensive view of the subject.

---

[17] For a company without debt, the manager's compensation is $s \times EV$, where s is the manager's participation ($(1 − s)$ is shareholders' participation). When the company takes on debt, the manager's compensation becomes $s[EV − (1 + r_L)L]$. For both equations to be equal, it is necessary that $s' > s$.

Bankruptcy costs

When bankruptcy is imminent, the company must confront a series of legal and administrative expenses. The bankruptcy procedure involves the hiring of lawyers and accounting experts. Even if bankruptcy is avoided, the reorganization of the company will demand new expenditures. As these expenses are financed with the firm's cash flows, the shareholders are harmed.

A central insight to bear in mind is that *it is not default risk but its associated costs which affect the total value of the firm, and in particular the shareholders' profit.* Let us suppose that the firm has a project of $100 financed with debt providing a cash flow of $80 with a probability of 50 per cent and $150 with identical probability. The required return is 10 per cent, and the corresponding interest rate is 40 per cent. If bankruptcy does not imply any expense at all (as we have supposed in previous sections), the expected value of the firm is $115 ($0.50 \times \$80 + 0.50 \times \$150 = \$115$), which is distributed between the shareholder and the lender as follows:

$$E\pi = 0.5 \times \$0 + 0.5 \times (\$150 - \$100 \times 1.40) = \$5$$
$$EI_{Lender} = 0.5 \times \$80 + 0.5 \times \$100 \times 1.40 = \$110$$

Note that, if the project were financed with internal funds the firm, by definition, would not go into bankruptcy, and shareholders would receive the whole $115 with the same $5 profit. Conversely, if default implies a cost of, say, $10 in legal and administrative expenses, the new expected value of the firm will be $110 [$0.50 \times (\$80 - \$10) + 0.50 \times \$150 = \$110$]. As this is the amount demanded by the creditors, the shareholder does not receive any money at all.[18]

How do shareholders pay for bankruptcy costs? Naturally, since these costs do not materialize except in the bad event, lenders charge a higher interest rate beforehand to make up for the resulting expenses. If we assume that bankruptcy costs are a lump sum b, the interest rate is defined by:

$$(1 + r)L = \alpha_s(1 + r_L) + \alpha_f(CF_f - b)$$
$$(1 + r_L) = \frac{(1 + r)L - \alpha_f(CF_f - b)}{\alpha_s L}$$

With our previous assumptions the interest rate will climb to 50 per cent and, as stated above, the shareholder profit goes to zero [$0.5 \times 0 + 0.5 \times (\$150 - \$100 \times 1.50) = 0$].[19]

In practice, *direct bankruptcy costs* are low. According to Altman (1984), they represent on average 3 per cent of the value of the firm, so it is difficult to attribute a heavy weight in financing decisions to them. However, bankruptcy risk involves other *indirect costs*, a deterioration in the capacity of running the business. Suppliers and buyers are reluctant to

---

[18] By the way, the equivalence between maximizing the shareholder's interests and maximizing the total value of the company (which comprises the value flowing to both shareholders and lenders) can be noted in this example: the value of the firm falls $5 and the wealth of the shareholders falls in the same magnitude.

[19] The reader should have noticed that this reasoning is similar to the analysis of monitoring costs in chapter 1. However, in that case the auditing reflects the unreliability of the firm's cash flow announcement, while here there is no informational asymmetry but just legal and accounting costs to transfer the assets from the incumbent shareholders to the lenders who gain possession of them.

operate with a financially distressed firm. Suppliers are afraid of getting unpaid credits, while consumers are likely to think that the company may relax its quality standards. Computing these indirect costs, the total costs of bankruptcy increase, according to some studies, to 20 per cent of the value of the firm.

If the company had been financed with stock or with retained earnings, bankruptcy would not have taken place, to the relief of shareholders. As bankruptcy takes place only because of the existence of debt with repayment risk, the company and its shareholders will benefit if the ratio of debt to equity is lower.

Taxes and capital structure

Even when there are no information problems, capital structure can influence the value of the company as long as the company, its shareholders and creditors pay taxes. Firms are taxed on their earnings *after* interest. For tax purposes, interest payments are considered an operating expense and, as such, are deductible. Let us see through a numerical example how debt and interest affect the return to shareholders. Since this issue is not strictly related to any information problems, we shall rule them out by assuming that the debt is safe. The project has a known value of $180 before taxes and interest and the lender's required return is 10 per cent. Assuming that the corporate tax rate is $t_c = 0.2$ and interest is deductible, the profit will amount to:

$$E\pi = EV - [EV - r_L \times L] \times t_c - (1 + r_L)L$$
$$= EV(1 - t_c) + r_L \times L \times t_c - (1 + r_L)L$$
$$= \$180 \times 0.8 + 0.1 \times \$100 \times 0.2 - 1.1 \times \$100 = \$36$$

As a result of the tax treatment to the interest payments, this profit is higher than the one attainable in case of financing the project with internal funds with the same opportunity cost, $r = 10$ per cent:

$$E\pi = EV \times (1 - t_c) - (1 + r)IF = \$34$$

Interestingly, this argument against the irrelevance of capital structure was put forward by Modigliani and Miller shortly after their most famous proposition. Their claim was that interest deductibility turns borrowing attractive by increasing the shareholder return without any change on the assets side.

However, the theory predicts very high debt to equity ratios, an inference which is far from matching the evidence. The existence of personal taxes is likely to reconcile, at least in part, theory and practice. Although interest payments are exempt at the corporate level, they are not at the personal one, as the lender must pay taxes on his interest income. Since the lender requires a net return of 10 per cent, he will translate the tax burden to the gross interest rate (the rate before taxes). If the personal tax rate is, say, 20 per cent, $t_p = 0.2$, the gross interest rate r_L is defined by:

$$r = rL \times (1 - t_p)$$
$$r_L = 0.125$$

Table 3.12 *Optimal leverage: decision variables*

In favour of high leverage	p.
Principal–agent problems	3.5
Tax advantage of debt	3.6

Against high leverage	Section
Adverse selection	3.3
Moral hazard	3.4
Bankruptcy costs	3.6

In the case that $t_c = t_p$, the previous tax advantage is completely offset by the higher interest rate charged by the lender:

$$E\pi = EV(1 - t_c) + r_L \times L \times t_c - (1 + r_L)L$$
$$= EV(1 - t_c) + [r/(1 - t_p)] \times L \times t_c - [1 + r/(1 - t_p)]L$$
$$= EV(1 - t_c) - (1 + r)L = \$34$$

In sum, the presence of taxes gives too drastic an answer to the choice between debt and capital: if the corporate tax rate is higher (lower) than the personal one, the firm should rely exclusively on debt (capital). Of course, we do not observe such extreme situations in the real world, which suggests that this is just one of the variables taken into account to decide the optimal financing structure.

3.7 Discussion

We have analysed a good many factors that may have an impact on a company's capital structure, i.e. that maximizes the total value of the firm. It has become clear that asymmetric information problems exert a central influence on this type of decision. We can list the factors that we considered in the chapters for and against a high level of debt in relation to capital (table 3.12).

Note that adverse selection creates a preference for retained earnings ahead of debt and stock, while in the other cases the contrast is between debt and capital as a whole (retained earnings and shares). Given the difficulty of quantifying these factors accurately, each company makes its global evaluation, often subjective, to determine the capital structure that maximizes the shareholders' wealth. The studies on this topic have traced some general rules that are derived from these principles, which real-world firms seem to follow:

(1) The higher the earnings, the lower the debt to equity ratio. With higher earnings, the company can rely on retained earnings ahead of the most expensive external sources.

(2) The higher the expected growth, the lower the debt to equity ratio. A company with valuable investment opportunities will prefer to maintain a low level of indebtedness and not have to share its earnings with creditors in the future.

(3) The more stable the cash flows and the larger the company, the higher the debt to equity ratio. These two variables imply that the probability of bankruptcy is low, which means that the associated costs are avoided.

(4) The higher the proportion of tangible assets, the higher the debt to capital ratio. Tangible assets (equipment, buildings) serve as collateral, which reduce the preference for risky projects and diminish the creditors' loss in the event of bankruptcy. In contrast, intangible assets (for example, R&D, trademarks) generally have a low resale value and are likely to become obsolete if the company goes into bankruptcy.

Bibliography

Altman, E. (1984) 'A further empirical investigation of the bankruptcy cost question', *Journal of Finance*, September.

A precise, empirical measurement of direct and indirect bankruptcy costs.

Bebczuk, R. (1999), *Essays in Corporate Saving, Financial Development, and Growth*, unpublished doctoral thesis, University of Illinois at Urbana-Champaign.

Chapter 2 offers calculations about the corporate financing structure in various OECD and Latin American countries.

Beck, T., A. Demirgüç–Kunt and V. Maksimor (2002), 'Financing patterns around the world: the role of institutions', Washington, DC: World Bank, mimeo.

New data on financing decisions with econometric work explaining them.

Copeland, T. and J. Weston (1988), *Financial Theory and Corporate Policy*, Reading, MA: Addison-Wesley.

A corporate finance textbook that combines mathematical rigour and intuition with a detailed presentation on the theory of corporate financing.

Harris, M. and A. Raviv (1991), 'The theory of capital structure', *Journal of Finance*, 46(1), 297–355.

An exhaustive summary of the models on the different theories of corporate capital structure and their empirical results.

Modigliani, F. and M. Miller (1958), 'The cost of capital, corporation finance, and the theory of investment', *American Economic Review*, 48(3), 261–97.

The pioneering article that opened the hotly debated topic of corporate financing.

Myers, S. (1984), 'The capital structure puzzle', *Journal of Finance*, 39(3), 575–91.

A sharp presentation about the determinants of corporate financing.

Myers, S. and N. Majluf (1984), 'Corporate financing and investment decisions when firms have information that investors do not have', *Journal of Financial Economics*, 13, 187–221.

An original elaboration on the pecking order theory.

Rajan, R. and L. Zingales (1995), 'What do we know about capital structure? Some evidence from international data', *Journal of Finance*, 50(5), 1421–60.

An analysis of the empirical determinants of financial decisions based on a thorough accounting analysis of a wide set of listed companies in developed countries.

Ritter, J. and I. Welsh (2002), 'A review of IPO activity, pricing, and allocations', *Journal of Finance*, 47, 1795–1828.

A comprehensive survey on theories and stylized facts in the IPO moment.

4 Asymmetric information and dividend policy

The study of dividend policy is an especially active area of debate in both the world of finance as well as the academic arena. Such interest is fully justified. In view of the relationship between dividends and stock prices, the topic is crucial for understanding both the primary stock market – where new issues of shares are carried out – and the secondary stock market – in which shares already in circulation are negotiated. From the perspective of the finance manager, a false impression could be created that the only relevant market is the primary one, ignoring that liquidity – the ability to transfer an asset at any moment – encourages demand for all financial instruments. Last but not least, in chapter 3 we emphasized that retained earnings are the main source of investment financing, and the volume of retained earnings depends not only on the availability of cash flows but also on the dividend policy of the firm.

As part of our treatment, we shall try to clarify some confusing ideas that surround dividend analysis. For example, it is commonly stated that a shareholder should feel attracted toward those stocks providing high dividends. We shall prove that if information problems are ignored such an assertion is as convincing as it is false. To spur the reader's curiosity, let us jump to the final conclusion now: for tax reasons, the shareholder benefits if the company does not distribute dividends at all. However, countering this, information problems *do* make it desirable for the company to disburse dividends.

4.1 Dividend policy in the world

To give more substance to our discussion we will take a look at the data in table 4.1, which displays retained earnings over total earnings in individual countries (sometimes referred to as **retention ratio**).

The figures in table 4.1 do not allow us to identify a clear pattern at the international level. Nevertheless, one can observe that in Latin America a minimal portion is distributed (in all cases, less than 15 per cent), while in the developed countries the **payout ratio** (dividends over earnings) is invariably higher than 50 per cent of earnings.

Before we discuss this further, the difference between **cash dividends**, **stock dividends** and **share repurchases** must be made clear. Our discussion will centre on cash dividends, representing a transfer of money from the firm to its shareholders. Stock dividends are

Table 4.1 *The retention ratio[a] in selected countries*

Country	Retained earnings/Total earnings
Developed countries	
United States	0.457
Japan	0.414
Germany	0.168
United Kingdom	0.212
Latin America	
Argentina	0.867
Chile	0.949
Colombia	0.911
Mexico	0.973
Venezuela	0.956

Note: [a]Information as of 1994.
Source: Rojas-Suarez and Weisbrod (1997).

Table 4.2 *Dividends and share repurchases in the 1,000 largest companies in the United States, 1973–1991 (per cent)*

Period	Dividends over earnings[a]	Repurchases over earnings[a]	Repurchases over dividends
1973–80	37.8	4.3	11.5
1981–91	51.4	27.5	53.3

Note: [a]Earnings before extraordinary items
Source: Allen and Michaely (1995).

nothing more than an illusion, since the shareholder receives new shares but no cash. This 'cosmetics' accounting leaves both assets and net equity unaffected. Lastly, the repurchase of shares by the firm from its own shareholders is conceptually equivalent to a cash dividend. The previous data take into account cash dividends omitting, for lack of statistical information, share repurchases. Share repurchases have experienced explosive growth since 1980, becoming a form of cash distribution comparable to the most traditional dividends. Table 4.2 shows, for the 1,000 largest companies in the United States, a significant increase in dividends payments, and an even more impressive jump in share repurchases.

4.2   The irrelevance of dividend policy

In absence of taxes and information problems, the dividend policy is irrelevant. This conclusion is undoubtedly controversial. The reasoning is the same one used in relation to the irrelevance of capital structure: if earnings generated by the company do not change, it should not matter if today's dividends are low and tomorrow's high, or vice versa. Modigliani

$D_0 = \$100$ $D_1 = \$30$

Year 0   Year 1

Figure 4.1   High present dividend: 1

and Miller elaborated this proposition too, in a (1961) article. The idea behind it is that if a company pays low dividends today but high ones tomorrow, the shareholder who wants high dividends today can sell some shares in the marketplace in order to increase present return. Naturally, when reducing stock holdings, future dividends will decrease. In the case that paid dividends are high today and low tomorrow, the shareholder who prefers the opposite can lend current excess dividends, which will provide him with high cash flows when the loan is repaid. To understand this point, we will develop a numerical example, adopting the following notation:

$$P = \text{Price}$$
$$D = \text{Dividends}$$
$$CG = \text{Capital gains}$$
$$r = \text{Required return}$$

For simplicity, let us assume that there is no uncertainty, which means that there is no asymmetric information either. The company in question has $100 available, which can be devoted to the payment of dividends to shareholders or to a productive project that offers an income of $140. The project is undertaken today (Year 0) and matures in one year (Year 1). If the firm opts to distribute dividends, it can request a loan at 10 per cent and take on the project anyway, creating the dividend profile in figure 4.1.

The dividends in the Year 0 ($100) are higher than in Year 1 ($30 = \$140 - \$100 \times (1.10)$.[1]

Although we have not previously spoken formally of the concept of **discount**, we have used it implicitly. Obtaining $30 today is not the same thing as receiving $30 in one year, since placing $30 in the bank at 10 per cent today would give us $33 next year. This is the reasoning we have followed so far. Instead of expressing the quantities in terms of future values, we can discount future cash flows to **present value**. To find the present value of $30 to be received in one year, we should make the following calculation:

$$(\text{Present value of } \$30) \times 1.10 = \$30$$
$$(\text{Present value of } \$30) = \$30/1.10 = \$27.3$$

The concept of discount is important because the market price of a share is the discount sum of dividends. The price that an investor will be willing to pay today (Year 0) for this

---

[1] The firm could also issue shares to finance the project. By issuing debt and lowering retained earnings, the debt to equity ratio increases, but it does not affect the results in the perfect capital market presented by Modigliani and Miller.

Figure 4.2   High future dividend: 2

share, before the dividend is paid in Year 0, is then:

$$P_0 \; = \; D_0 + D_1/1.10 \; = \; \$100 + \$30/1.10 \; = \; \$127.3$$

Under the second alternative, we have the dividend profile in figure 4.2.

Now the company does not pay any dividend in Year 0, but it compensates shareholders with a higher one in Year 1. In spite of the change in the time pattern of dividends, the stock price is the same as before:

$$P_0 \; = \; D_0 + D_1 \, (1 + r)$$
$$= \; \$0 + \$140/1.10 \; = \; \$127.3$$

The company's fundamentals, as reflected in its productive projects (cash flows of $100 in Year 0 and $140 in Year 1) and the cost of capital (10 per cent), are the same under the two possible scenarios, and so is the value of the firm. Therefore, the moment at which cash flows are transferred to the shareholders – the dividend policy – is trivial.

The reader may wonder why a potential investor would be indifferent between buying, before the payment of a dividend in Year 0, a stock that pays an attractive dividend and one that pays absolutely nothing. The missing link in this story is the existence of **capital gains**. An investor can obtain profitability either through dividends or the sale of stock at a price higher than the one at which he purchased it in the first place, the difference being the capital gain. To analyse the relation among price, dividends and capital gains, let us suppose that the company disappears after Year 1. In this light, we can define the required return r as:

$$r \; = \; [D_0 + CG_0]/P_0 \; = \; [D_0 + (P_1 - P_0)]/P_0$$

This equality can also be expressed as:

$$1 + r \; = \; [D_0 + P_1]/P_0$$

which states that the return to the shareholder is just the ratio between income (dividends and selling price) and cost (purchasing price). Under the policy of high current dividend and low future dividend, this formula takes the following values:

$$1.10 \; = \; (\$100 + P_1)/\$127.3$$

from where the price in Year 1, after paying the dividend in Year 0, is:

$$P_1 \; = \; \$127.3 \times 1.10 - \$100 \; = \; \$40$$

We can already calculate the gain (in this case, loss) of capital, $P_1 - P_0 = -\$87.3$ ($\$40 - \$127.3 = -\$87.3$). The price falls abruptly to $40 owing to the previous distribution of dividends. To check that this procedure is correct, we should find that this combination of dividends and capital gains yields a return of 10 per cent:

$$r = [D_0 + GC]/P_0 = (\$100 - \$87.3)/127.3 = 0.10$$

We can repeat the calculation for the case in which $D_0 = \$0$ and $D_1 = \$140$. The price in Year 1, P_1, becomes:

$$1.10 = (\$0 + P_1)/\$127.3$$
$$P_1 = \$127.3 \times 1.10 - \$0 = \$140$$

This price just reflects the dividends to be received in Year 1. The capital gain is now $12.7 ($\$140 - \$127.3 = \$12.7$) and the return is once again 10 per cent:

$$r = [D + CG]/P_0 = (\$0 + \$12.7)/127.3 = 0.10$$

In summary, for a given amount of earnings over the life of a company, high current dividends are compensated by capital losses to the point of making the dividend policy insignificant.

4.3   Taxes and dividend policy

Paying taxes is not only unpleasant but also complicated. To elaborate, in section 4.2 we declined to mention that the firm's cash flows are subject to double taxation, first at the corporate level and then at the shareholder level when she receives dividends. As a result, financial economists argue that shareholders benefit if the company does not distribute any dividend, since they avoid this second tax. This recommendation contrasts with the intuition that links stock profitability and dividends, but we have offered compelling reasons against it once capital gains enter the scene – the tax disadvantage of dividends actually resides in the fact that the tax rate on dividends is higher than that on capital gains.

We shall rewrite the previous formulas to add this tax effect, using the following additional notation:

$$E = \text{Equity issue}$$
$$t_D = \text{Tax rate on dividends}$$
$$t_{CG} = \text{Tax rate on capital gains}$$

The company can follow alternative strategies:

(1) Pay $100 worth of dividends and issue equity for another $100 in order to take on the project in Year 0, and pay dividends of $140 in Year 1
(2) Reinvest the original $100 in Year 0 and pay dividends of $140 in Year 1.

$D_0 = \$100$
$E_0 = \$100$ $D_1 = \$140$

Year 0   Year 1

Figure 4.3   High present dividend: 2

$D_0 = \$0$ $D_1 = \$140$

Year 0   Year 1

Figure 4.4   High future dividend: 2

Graphically, the first strategy looks like that in figure 4.3.
The second looks like that in figure 4.4.
The stock price without taxes would be the same in both cases ($127.3). This is another example that demonstrates the irrelevance of the dividend policy. But it is no longer immaterial when taxes are integrated into the analysis. Let us suppose that the dividend tax is 20 per cent ($t_D = 20$ per cent) and the capital gains tax is 0 per cent ($t_{CG} = 0$ per cent). Bearing in mind that the company does not pay any tax for issuing shares, the price in Year 1 would be:[2]

$$P_0 = (1 - t_D)D_0 - E_0 + (1 - t_D)D_1/(1 + r)$$

We are now ready to calculate the stock price under the first strategy:

$$P_0 = (1 - 0.20) \times \$100 - \$100 + (1 - 0.20) \times \$140/(1.10) = \$81.8$$

and under the second:

$$P_0 = (1 - 0.20) \times \$140/(1.10) = \$101.8$$

Since the firm is financed exclusively with shares, these are the stockholders' discounted cash flows. As long as the company has good investment opportunities, it is clear that distributing dividends reduces the shareholder' wealth.[3] The reason is the increase of taxable revenue: under the first strategy, shareholders pay a tax of $20 (0.20 × $100 = $20) in Year 0 *and* a tax of $28 (0.20 × $140 = $28) in Year 1. On the other hand, under the second strategy, shareholders save $20 by reinvesting profits in the company. It is not coincidental, then, that the difference in P_0 between the alternatives is exactly $20.

---

[2] E_0 is substracted because an equity issue is a flow of money from shareholders to the firm, namely, the opposite of a dividend.
[3] If the firm does not have good investment opportunities – in our example, with an expected return higher than 10 per cent – it is convenient for it to distribute dividends when corporate tax is higher than personal tax.

4.4   The dividend puzzle and information problems

Until now we have found that the dividend policy is either irrelevant or harmful for the interests of the shareholders. However, in the financial business it is clear that, at least in developed countries, companies choose to pay substantial dividends. The figures on retention ratios in the world back this up. At the same time, several studies have reached two conclusions that reinforce the value that the market attaches to dividends:

(1) Companies avoid decreasing dividends from their historical values as much as possible.[4]
(2) The announcement of higher dividends increases the stock price.[5]

At first sight, the concern for high dividends seems unjustified. Not only are tax costs present, but it is also possible to transfer cash to shareholders by means of share repurchase transactions, which results in a much less onerous tax burden. Although share repurchases have been employed with growing intensity since the beginning of the 1970s, we have seen that dividends continue to be prominent. Another argument against dividends is that, in order to substitute self-financing, firms need to pay a higher cost of capital in the financial system when confronting asymmetric information and intermediation costs.

So, why are dividends distributed in spite of all these disadvantages? This is the 'dividend puzzle'. This puzzle has drawn the attention of many investigators, who arrived at several possible explanations:

The payment of dividends is a signal that conveys to the market good news on the firm's prospects

As we have just mentioned, companies try at all costs to avoid a reduction of dividends. Because of this, when they do decide to increase dividends, investors interpret these additional dividends to be permanent. If the dividend increase is thought to be permanent (as opposed to a redistribution over time of the same amount of dividends, as in the discussion in section 4.2), the market price will be higher, which in turn means that the cost of equity will be lower.

The important thing here is to remember the role that information problems play in this story. If these were not present, why would the company not simply announce higher earnings in the future and maintain previous dividend levels? The answer lies in the fact that shareholders dispute the truthfulness of these announcements, considering it 'cheap talk'. The management's superior information in comparison to its shareholders, who do not know in detail what happens inside the firm, reduces the credibility of any announcement not involving a real commitment (such as a dividend increase).

Our discussion in section 2.2 about the value of information signals is also pertinent here, but with a twist. When referring earlier to collateral and internal funds, the signal

---

[4] For example, on a sample of more than 1,800 American companies, Allen and Michaely (1995) found that in 1993, 86.6 per cent of the companies maintained previous dividends, 7.3 per cent increased them and 6.0 per cent reduced them.

[5] Allen and Michaely (1995) showed that, on average, an increase in dividends resulted in a stock price up 0.4 per cent while a decrease produced a fall of 1.3 per cent. Meanwhile, the introduction of a dividend caused an average stock price increase of 3 per cent while an interruption caused a fall of 7 per cent.

was intended to contend with asymmetric information today, the goal being to obtain better financial conditions when applying for the *present* project. Instead, dividends act as a signal to reduce the cost of capital on *future* projects.[6] In the latter case, the cost of the signal is that, upon giving up internal funds, the company imposes on itself the extra cost of resorting to the more expensive external sources of funding. This decision to 'burn money' can actually be a revenue-yielding strategy if it allows the firm to gain credibility and facilitate its access to capital markets in the future.

To illustrate the point, let us reconsider the case examined in section 4.3, in which the firm must decide between the self-financing and the dividend/equity issue alternatives. Unlike that case, let us ignore taxes and give room again to asymmetric information in the form of adverse selection. Moreover, suppose that internal funds are available at a cost of 10 per cent and equity, owing to the undervaluation of good projects, at a cost of 20 per cent. To minimize the cost of capital for the current project, the entrepreneur should be inclined to use retained earnings, but in the face of valuable investment opportunities in the future, she might prefer distributing such earnings and issuing new equity. This will naturally reduce her present profit, but the payment of the promised high dividends will probably ease the access to future equity funding at a much lower cost than 20 per cent, provided the market perceives that this is a high-productivity firm.

For this strategy to pay off, it is necessary not only that this firm (the type *A* firm) has many good future projects but that the signal is effective, namely, low-productivity firms (type *B*) competing for funding find it unprofitable to follow the same path. Otherwise, firms seemingly similar in the eyes of potential investors will be treated in the same way financially, regardless of their differential intrinsic quality.

For instance, this will happen if the *B* firm has a low expected value, which makes it impossible to cover a 20 per cent cost of capital ($I > P$, where as always I is the initial investment and P is the common value attached to both project *A* and *B*). Alternatively, if the *B* firm has to service previous debts, its shareholders may be unable to get any money even with a higher expected value.

In sum, firms will be willing to pay high and stable dividends as long as the current tax and financing costs are outweighed by the future benefits in terms of better financial conditions after informational barriers have been overcome.

The payment of dividends tends to mitigate agency conflicts
A second asymmetric information-related argument is that dividend payments help discipline managers pursuing personal goals, an issue especially relevant for companies with high current profitability and scarce investment opportunities, as can be the case for mature, successful companies. This is the *free cash flows* hypothesis, discussed in section 3.5.

By using such free cash flows to pay dividends, the discretionary power of management is partially put under control. Accordingly, dividends are interpreted by the market as good

---

[6] Notice that under this new perspective the use of internal funds, unlike what we saw in chapter 2, is no longer a good signal.

Year 0   Year 1

Figure 4.5 High present dividend: 3

Year 0   Year 1

Figure 4.6 High future dividend: 3

news, as shareholders can now invest the funds outside of the company to obtain a better return than by reinvesting them in the firm in projects yielding a high personal benefit for the manager but a low one for shareholders.

Many investors are reluctant to sell shares to obtain cash

This preference for dividends over capital gains arises because some investors consider the sale of stock, unlike dividends, to be wealth-reducing. This belief is understandable but not necessarily rational. Logically, selling shares to consume is counterproductive only if liquidating stock holdings today provides less money than receiving dividends over time. If the market is efficient, the stock price will properly reflect all future dividends, so that the investor should be indifferent between waiting for dividends or selling today. Given two stocks with equal potential earnings, one offering high dividends and the other low dividends, it is always possible to generate an identical cash flow from period to period; for the first share the primary source of cash will be dividends, for second it will be capital gains. Let us verify this through our earlier example (figures 4.5 and 4.6).

Let us suppose that our investor feels more comfortable with the first share: high dividends today but low ones tomorrow. The second, however, can offer the same cash revenue: since the initial price is $127.3, selling 78.5 per cent of the package provides $100 (0.785 × $127.3 = $100) in Year 0, while in Year 1 $30 in dividends are received from the remaining holdings (0.215 × $140 = $30).

Some investors favour the certainty of present dividends over the uncertainty of future dividends, this risk aversion makes the stock with high current dividends preferable[7]

Keep in mind that high present dividends do not make a share less risky than others with high future dividends: as we are dealing with the same productive project, cash dividends

---

[7] Let us remember that our analysis is based on risk neutral investors, unless we explicitly state otherwise. To be reminded of the difference between neutrality and risk aversion, return to section 1.1. In this particular case, risk aversion would take the form of a discount higher than 10 per cent, penalizing the postponement of dividend payments, and lowering the present value of the stock that offers low current and high future dividends.

in Year 1 will fluctuate in the same way under both strategies. This preference for current dividends would make sense only if the shareholder's discount rate were higher than the cost of capital because there is a compensation for risk, or *risk premium*. For instance, if the discount rate was 20 per cent instead of 10 per cent (the required return under risk neutrality), everything else constant, the stock price with high current dividends would be $125 (100 + $30/1.2 = $125), which is higher than the price of $116.7 ($140/1.2 = $116.7) of the share with high future dividends.

For certain groups of investors it is possible to counteract the tax disadvantage of dividends

For example, companies that acquire shares of other firms can deduct a portion of their dividends when paying taxes on profits, and institutional investors (pension funds, mutual funds, insurance companies) are generally exempt from paying taxes on dividends. In other cases, skilled accountants can find loopholes in the tax code allowing them to avoid paying the charge. In any of these situations, dividends will be neutral in terms of taxes and the advantages of dividends already discussed will become decisive.

4.5   Discussion

After considering the different factors that influence dividend policy, we see that the abundance of theories conceals the frustrating absence of a unified explanation on the topic. It is anyway irrefutable that, amid this intellectual avalanche, focusing on information problems is the most reputable explanation for the distribution of dividends in spite of the tax disadvantages and the existence of alternative channels to transfer profits to shareholders.

   To finish, it is interesting to go back to table 3.1 on retention ratios in the world (p. 39). There we pointed out that in Latin America a much smaller proportion of earnings is distributed than in most other advanced countries. We can offer a partial explanation based on the informational content of dividends. We have said that all companies want to demonstrate to their present and potential shareholders how healthy they are on productive and financial grounds. Dividend distribution is an unequivocal signal of solvency and profitability, but like all signals it is expensive. The cost in this case is that the company must substitute for the distributed cash new resources to take on its new projects. The limited development in financial markets in Latin America is reflected in the high cost of external financing sources (both in debt and stock) and, in some cases, in a complete lack of interest on the part of investors in financing firms by purchasing new equity issues – even without the high intermediation costs involved. Distributing dividends can thus make a firm financially unable to take on high revenue-yielding investments in the present, without the corresponding future benefit of getting low-cost stock funding in the future. Using this cost–benefit framework, it becomes clear why the informational value of dividends is not a especially relevant consideration for a great percentage of companies in this region.

Bibliography

Allen, F. and R. Michaely (1995), 'Dividend policy', *Handbook on Operational Research*, Amsterdam: Elsevier.
  An exhaustive report on the theory and evidence of dividend policy, mostly referring to the United States.
Bagwell, L. and J. Shoven (1989), 'Cash distributions to shareholders', *Journal of Economic Perspectives*, 3(3), 129–40.
  An informal presentation on the 'dividend puzzle', with special attention to the growing importance of share repurchases.
Baker, K., G. Powell and T. Veit (2002), 'Revisiting managerial perspectives on dividend policy', *Journal of Economics and Finance*, 26.
  A review of the different reasons to pay dividends supporting an original survey among NASDAQ companies.
La Porta, R., F. Lopez-de-Silanes, A. Shleifer and R. Vishny (1999), 'Agency problems and dividend policies around the world', Harvard University, mimeo.
  A thorough analysis of dividend policies and their tax treatment in thirty-nine countries.
Modigliani, F. and M. Miller (1961), 'Dividend policy, growth and the valuation of shares', *Journal of Business*, 34.
Rojas-Suarez, L. and S. Weisbrod (1997), 'Financial markets and the behaviour of private savings in Latin America', in R. Hausmann and H. Reisen (eds.), *Promoting Savings in Latin America*, Washington, DC: IDB/OFCD.
Ross, S., R. Westerfield and J. Jaffe (1996), *Corporate Finance*, 4th edn. New York: Irwin.
  Cited in chapter 1; chapter 18 is dedicated to dividend policy.

Part III   Macroeconomic applications

5 Asymmetric information, the financial system and economic growth

The presence of a financial system in the economic landscape of modern societies seems so natural that to question why it exists seems superfluous. However, the question is both relevant and appropriate. Enormous economic resources are devoted to setting and running the financial system, which captures more than 5 per cent of GDP in the majority of countries. How does society justify devoting such a colossal quantity of money to support a sector that does not provide any tangible product or increase directly the welfare of its citizens?

The financial system has the function of *intermediating between those who save and those in need of funds*. Let us imagine for a moment a society without an organized financial system. First, the saver would look for individuals in search of funds. Secondly, both would agree on the conditions of the loan. Thirdly, the saver would somehow verify that the borrower had a good project and was honest, and would take precautions to be sure that she would be repaid. Fourthly, the borrower would find enough savers to collect the amount of money needed for the project, repeating the first three steps as many times as necessary.

It is clear that there would be a very low probability for two individuals at random to find each other and to coincide in their needs and preferences. Even after overcoming that difficult round, let us estimate the costs involved in each operation and then multiply them by the millions of identical transactions that would take place daily in any economy. By agglomerating the savings of numerous individuals and specializing in the evaluation and monitoring of a great number of potential borrowers, the financial system helps to avoid a considerable waste of resources. We could even be tempted to restate our initial scepticism and wonder why the financial system is so inadequately remunerated! Luckily, the answer is simple: in a competitive economy each sector is compensated according to the value of its services, i.e. the financial sector's stake in GDP is high because of the high value that society places on it.

Using more technical language, the financial system aims at lowering *transaction costs* and *information costs*. **Transaction costs** are the expenses arising from the process of meeting, writing the contract and making the periodical payments. **Information costs** include the assessment of the project and the entrepreneur, and monitoring during the span of the contract.

We need to emphasize that *information costs minimize but do not eliminate information problems* – adverse selection, moral hazard and monitoring costs. Information costs consist

Figure 5.1   Financial intermediation process

of verifying the truthfulness and accuracy of information given by the debtor that has the objective of accumulating capital, and to supervising the debtor during the life of the project. Neither the estimation of cash flows nor the probability of success is trivial, so that the creditor's professionalism is extremely useful in making sure that the project is as good as the debtor claims. But the creditor will continue to be excluded from the realm of the debtor's private information. Dishonest intentions are never written on paper.

Since information problems are closely linked to the emergence and development of the financial system, and the latter affects the economic growth process, we shall discuss the connection among these topics that, until not long ago, were considered part of separate disciplines.

5.1   Functions of the financial system

The financial system includes a wide range of intermediaries, among them banks, investment funds, pension funds and insurance companies. In most of what follows, we shall refer to **banks**, but the analysis can easily be extended to other financial intermediaries.

In order to increase future consumption, people save part of their income and deposit such **savings** in a bank.[1] The financial institution lends those deposits to other individuals who, instead, want to spend beyond their current revenue. In chapters 1–3 we stressed this second operation by taking the bank as the lender. Now, we shall complete the analysis by introducing the actual, ultimate supplier of funds, that is, the saver (see figure 5.1).[2]

The importance of the financial system in the intermediation process proceeds from three factors:

(1) **Economies of scale**   Economies of scale exist when the *unit cost* falls as the scale or volume of transactions rises owing to the presence of fixed costs (costs that do not vary with the volume of production). Let us suppose that the creation of a bank requires a fixed cost of $100 in buildings and computer infrastructure plus staffing expenses. The cost of evaluating and monitoring each borrower is $10, representing a *variable cost* with the volume of production, in our case loans. The unit cost of a loan depends on

---

[1] Later on, we will show figures on how financial savings are distributed between bank and non-bank institutions.
[2] It should be clear that the investment here is a productive investment, not a financial one. Another comment: the financial system can also finance the consumption of some individuals, a point we set aside for now to concentrate on the productive side.

how many loans the bank carries out. If it makes a single loan, the unit cost will be:

$$\text{Unit cost} = (\text{Fixed costs} + \text{Variable costs})/\text{Number of loans}$$
$$\text{Unit cost} = (\$100 + \$10)/1 = \$110$$

If the bank grants two loans, the unit cost falls to:

$$\text{Unit cost} = (\$100 + \$10 \times 2)/2 = \$60$$

The same mechanism applies to deposits. Let us remember that in the absence of a bank, each lender/borrower would have to spend $110 on a loan. Two loans would imply an expense of $220 ($110 × 2 = $220), while with bank intermediation, the expense drops to $120 ($100 + $10 × 2 = $120). In this way society saves $100 in transaction and information costs that can be redirected to increasing consumption or investment.

(2) **Maturity matching** Generally, depositors want to part with their money for only a short time, while borrowers need funds for a more extended period, given that productive projects are usually long term. To reconcile these different preferences, banks take short-term deposits and grant long-term credits.

Term matching for clients creates term mismatching for the financial institution. If the depositor decides to withdraw the money after thirty days, but the bank has lent it for one year, it would not have enough cash to pay the deposit back. Nevertheless, when the number of clients is high, it is much less probable that all depositors will decide to withdraw their money at the same time – instead, it is likely that the withdrawals of some will be compensated by the deposits of others. On the basis of on historical experience, the bank is able roughly to predict the daily turnover of net deposits using statistical methods.

(3) **Risk matching** The typical saver is risk averse and wants to be sure that, after the agreed term has expired, she receives the initial capital plus interest.[3] The borrower, on the other hand, usually goes ahead with risky projects of high productivity (without which she would be unwilling to take on debt with interest). Additionally, information problems add to the normal risk of every project, paving the way for the borrower to exploit her informational advantage at the expense of the saver.

Financial entities are particularly good at diminishing the depositor's risk. As a first measure, they attenuate risks through **diversification**, namely, they lend to different firms and sectors, so that for some projects that fail, there are others that succeed. Also they place a portion of their deposits in cash and other liquid investments such as shares and bonds. By doing this, the bank not only removes the depositor's risk but also lowers the debtor's cost of capital. Diversification is as powerful an idea as it is

---

[3] Let us keep in mind that in the previous chapters we have broken away from risk aversion when postulating that the financial system as well as the debtors were neutral to risk (see section 1.1). Although we could maintain that assumption, the most significant point is the aversion to risk of depositors. We will return to this point in chapters 7 and 8.

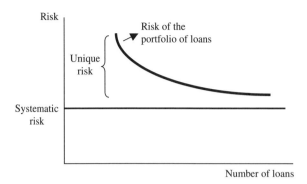

Figure 5.2   Total risk

simple.[4] However, its correct implementation demands a professional experience that the individual depositor lacks. This same notion holds for the compilation and processing of information regarding a potential borrower. Although information provided may be trustworthy, a project contains economic and technical specifications that exceed the average depositor's knowledge. In some cases, information may not be reliable, and it is there that the experience and specialization of the financier is irreplaceable to detect fraud or to prevent its consequences.

Nonetheless, the bank cannot eliminate all risk. All loans (and all assets in general) possess two sources of risk: unique risk and systematic risk. **Unique risk** is particular to the project in question, while **systematic risk** is common to all loans. Let us think of a catastrophe that affects the whole economy: regardless of the risk of each firm's fundamentals (the quality of its managers, its leverage, input costs, product demand), a widespread disaster would have a massive and unavoidable impact on the system as a whole.

When not perfectly correlated, a loan portfolio will be less risky as the number of borrowers increases through efficient diversification, but systemic risk is non-diversifiable. It is possible to represent this idea in the following way:

$$\text{Total risk} = \text{Systematic risk} + \text{Unique risk}$$
$$\downarrow \text{Diversification}$$
$$\text{Total risk} = \text{Systematic risk}$$

Or, graphically as in figure 5.2.

---

[4] James Tobin, whom we will mention again in chapter 6, received the Nobel Prize in economics in 1981 partly for his contributions to the study of diversification in the 1950s. Tobin has been an involuntary victim of the simplicity of the concept. Upon receiving the Nobel Prize, journalists asked him to explain his findings. His presentation, somewhat technical, did not satisfy the press who desired a brief summary intelligible for the general public; Tobin responded with the adage: 'Don't put all your eggs in one basket.' The following day newspapers sarcastically suggested that an economist had won no less than the Nobel Prize simply by presenting a piece of common knowledge as an economic discovery. A newspaper even printed, next to the news, a cartoon in which the next winner of the Nobel Prize in medicine appeared relating his award-winning findings: 'An apple a day keeps the doctor away.'

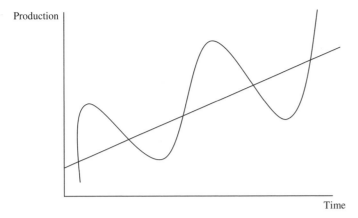

Production

Time

Figure 5.3   Short- and long-term growth

5.2   An introduction to economic growth

We could not appreciate the significance of information problems in financial markets for the development of countries if we did not understand the process and determinants of economic growth. Growth theory is the branch of economics that studies the causes of long-term growth in *per capita* product. If we were to identify the economist's main concern, it would be growth. The ultimate objective of politics and the science of economics is to maximize the public's welfare, which to a large extent depends on the quantity of goods and services that they consume; since economic growth is the only way to increase the availability of goods and services, the nexus between growth and welfare is established.

The basic inputs of production are *labour and physical capital* – machinery, plant and infrastructure. Since labour increases both production and population, the main motor of productivity growth *per capita* is physical capital. More important still, the innovation of new ideas and production processes generates growth through *technological progress* by improving the quality of capital and labour. These advances make intensive use of *human capital*, the creative capacity of individuals whose foundation lies in education and training.

A clear distinction should be made between **short-** and **long-term growth**. All economies are subject to adverse situations that temporarily reduce production below optimal output given the amount of available productive resources. A great drought, low exports or a period of political uncertainty can cause unemployment and capital idleness. The policies designed to overcome this unfavourable situation – among them, increased public expenditures, devaluation or an increase in the money supply – tend to stimulate *short-term growth* via an increase in aggregate *demand*. For example, when building a new road, the government can employ inactive resources, raising production volume without adding new capital or more labour. When *full employment* is recovered, the increase in demand for a fixed quantity of goods and services creates inflationary pressures. In the graph in figure 5.3, we are worried about the determinants of long-term trend (the straight line), postponing the analysis of short-run economic cycles (the waves around the straight line) until chapter 6.

The only way to achieve long-run growth is to increase the *supply* of productive inputs. A choice must then be made between present consumption and future consumption. To increase the quantity of physical and human capital it is necessary to save a fraction of current income to conduct those investment activities. A hedonistic attitude of consuming without replenishing capital today will deprive society of future consumption. In a society with many individuals, some will want to be borrowers of funds and others will become lenders. As we have seen, reconciling these two sectors would be chaotic and expensive without the financial system. In section 5.4 we shall present some figures on the sources of economic growth and how they affect the financial system.

5.3   The financial system and economic growth

Grounded on the concepts developed in sections 5.1 and 5.2, we are ready to figure out the link between economic growth and the financial system. A country can grow in the long run by increasing both the **quantity** and **quality** of investment and the financial system influences both channels:

(1) **The financial system raises the quantity of investment**   In an economy without access to international credit, saving equals investment. To see this equivalence, let us remember that income can be used for either consumption or investment:

$$\text{Income} = \text{Consumption} + \text{Investment}$$

In turn, savings is defined as the difference between income and consumption, and we immediately arrive at the identity Saving = Investment:

$$\text{Income} - \text{Consumption} = \text{Saving} = \text{Investment}$$

However, those who save are not always those who invest. Aligning these two groups causes, as seen before, transaction and information costs, which reduce the amount of money actually devoted to investment:

$$\text{Investment} = \text{Savings} - (\text{Transaction and information costs})$$

Because of economies of scale, the financial system makes the intermediation process much more efficient, lowering the transaction and information costs and raising investment and growth.

(2) **The financial system increases the quality of investment**   The more productive investments are risky and illiquid – the hunger for profits rapidly eliminates safe and profitable opportunities. This implies in many cases large sums of money placed in projects of long maturation and uncertain results, a good example being R&D expenses. The average saver is averse to risk and illiquidity, and thus prefers to invest in safe instruments. In the extreme cases where the financial system does not offer sufficient security, savers will prefer to maintain their money on hand (under the mattress or in the sugar bowl) or to invest it in property or in a new car. Funds placed in these low- or nill-productivity activities will deprive many innovative managers of the necessary funds

to realize their projects. Technological progress, and thus growth, will be extremely slow. Therefore, the intercession of the financial system, which creates a financial asset (deposit) that satisfies the saver's demands and creates a financial tool (loan) that fills the needs of entrepreneurs, impels economic growth.

It is important to note that the financial intermediary does not eliminate or absorb all risk. What it does is to *reduce* the risk by means of professional handling of the funds, using as tools diversification and the evaluation and control of borrowers. It does not absorb depositor risk either: if there is a global catastrophe that affects the whole loan portfolio, diversification is no longer effective and it is the depositor, not the bank, who suffers the losses. In chapter 7, we shall analyse these *financial crises*.

No less important is the role of the financial system in selecting the most promising projects among the numerous applicants who desire financing. Even if savers were not risk averse, they would not possess the capacity or the necessary knowledge to choose the best projects. Conversely, the financial intermediary does have the means and ability to do this, without technical complexity or geographic location constituting an insolvable impediment.

As we concluded in chapter 2, the stock market has more incentives to choose profitable projects because shareholders receive a given fraction of total cash flows. Banks have a natural bias toward the most conservative projects because they want only to minimize the risk of losing the agreed-upon capital and interest. In spite of their preference for projects of moderate risk, the role of banks in the growth process should not be downplayed. Banks have a comparative advantage in comparison to other intermediaries in alleviating information problems. In countries where stock markets are not developed, banks constitute the only source of external financing; in those where they are, access to bank credit is interpreted favourably by the market and can be the gateway to a successful stock issue. Banks also impose discipline on owners and managers and hence improve productive efficiency by way of threatening the interruption of credit and the consequences of financial distress.[5] On the other hand, banks often acquire stock packages as part of their diversification policy and to improve the overall liquidity of their portfolios, thus contributing to the financing of riskier projects.[6]

The financial system also improves the quality of investment when it reduces the **liquidity** needs of companies and overcomes the **indivisibility** of some investments. During the life of a productive project expenses accrue, such as the payment of administrative wages,

---

[5] These issues have been treated in chapter 3; we said that it is possible to find the optimal capital structure, a mixture of debt and stock that creates the necessary incentives for the company to choose the best investments. Naturally, the best investments for the company are, in most cases, the best investments for the country as a whole.

[6] The authorities trying to avoid excessive portfolio risk also limit bank intervention in the stock market. In some industrial countries, such as Germany, the United Kingdom, Italy and the Netherlands, banks have more freedom in this sense. In particular in Germany, banks usually lead initial public offerings of companies (*underwriting*) and acquiring shares of industrial companies. This market orientation of banks has been called *universal banking*. Another peculiar case is the Japanese *keiretsu*, industrial groups that generally include a large bank. By being a direct or indirect shareholder of affiliated companies a bank has more incentive to finance risky projects, as it has an evident information advantage. It remains to be seen if depositors are harmed by this bond between bank and company. Similar cases in Latin America at the end of the 1970s and beginning of the 1980s, and in Asia in the 1990s, make this a pressing discussion.

rent and taxes. To cover these expenses, the company must maintain cash and other liquid assets, components of working capital that do not directly contribute to productivity. Some of these resources can be dedicated to productive investments when the financial system flows smoothly.

Let us suppose that a company can invest in a project that generates 1 unit of production for every $10 invested; the company has $100, but during the development process it must pay wages and taxes of $20. If credit does not exist, it will barely be able to invest $80 and produce 8 units, maintaining the rest in cash to make those payments, while with credit it could invest $100 and produce 10 units, temporarily incurring debt of $20 to pay the expenses. The presence of the financial system allows production to be raised by 2 units. Equally important, unexpected expenses might come up in the development of the project, so in the absence of readily available credit, a liquid buffer stock would have to be maintained, siphoning resources from productive investments. Otherwise, illiquidity may be very costly, even causing good projects to be prematurely terminated.

A notorious characteristic of many of highly productive projects is *indivisibility*. The last example is of a divisible project: the manager could invest $10 and produce 1 unit, or invest $100 and produce 10 units. An indivisible project is one in which an investment, lower than, say, $100 is not possible. This situation is more realistic when a new project is begun: it is not possible to buy and install, let us say, a third of a machine. In our example, a manager with $70 of internal funds and without external financing would have to decline the lucrative project. Credit again helps to overcome the problem of indivisibility by promoting higher production and growth.

Finally, we must not fail to mention that the financial system facilitates the **accumulation of human capital**. Education is expensive, in both terms of tuition and materials, and because it takes away time available for work. Borrowing allows individuals (or parents) with scarce funds to finance this kind of investment. Credit for education still suffers sharper information problems than productive investments, especially since the financed 'asset' – the person obtaining education – is not seizable, provided a slave regime does not exist!

This is the right moment to summarize our findings up to this point and connect the present chapter with previous ones. We have gone from a microeconomic perspective, focused on the relationship between individual borrowers and lenders, to a macroeconomic perspective, based on the aggregate of all companies and the financial system as a whole. However, the essence of the analysis has not changed. National investment is nothing but the sum of all investments I, and the gross domestic product, or GDP, is the sum of all cash flows CF obtained by their respective projects. The different conclusions that we have come to can be summarized through our familiar equation:

$$E\pi = EV - \alpha_s(1 + r_L)L$$

The financial system elevates the quality of the investment, measured by EV, and reduces the interest rate r_L, increasing in both cases the expected profit $E\pi$. In a capitalist economy, fuelled by the economic incentives of the private sector, the bigger the profit, the bigger the investment and growth. Certainly, the demand for funds for investment increases, but what about supply? It may not be always true that a reduction in the interest rate discourages savings; on the contrary when information problems and transaction costs are alleviated it is possible that the interest rate received by depositors will actually increase. In section 5.4 we shall also see that a higher interest rate does not guarantee larger savings.

5.4   Saving decisions and the financial system

The financial system can also affect national saving. First, financial intermediaries specialize in finding profitable investment opportunities and therefore pay depositors an attractive interest rate. The higher the interest rate, the bigger the incentive to save or, in other words, to substitute present consumption for future consumption. Acting against this **substitution effect** there is an **income effect**: by investing at a higher interest rate, savers increase their future income and spend more today (save less). On the whole, the interest rate has an ambiguous effect on saving. As a matter of fact, the empirical evidence supports this inconclusive effect by finding a small, or in some cases nil, response in the saving rate (saving over GDP) to the interest rate.

Secondly, individuals usually save more as uncertainty over the future rises, since they try to cover themselves against adverse shocks by building a 'buffer stock'. This saving motive is referred to as **precautionary saving**. For example, a worker expecting to be laid off in the next year will save a larger percentage of his income this year to avoid an abrupt fall in consumption if he is indeed fired. The financial system reduces the saver's uncertainty by allowing him to obtain a loan to avoid the fall in consumption until a new job is found. As a result, precautionary saving will be lower. The evidence on this point is mixed, but the rationale is still sound.

Finally, the financial system can also reduce saving incentives when relaxing **financial constraints**, a topic about which we shall speak in detail in chapter 6. A firm or a consumer suffers financial constraints when they cannot borrow as much as they could in a well-functioning capital market. When external sources of funds are not available, these individuals will need to save more in advance to carry out their investment plans. As the financial system develops and financial constraints are less stringent, the saving rate may become lower.

Let us think of an individual with an income of $100 who wants to buy a new car for $50. Without the option of credit, this person will cut consumption (for example, he will take a shorter holiday) to be able to buy the car. He will spend $50 and save the remaining $50 to buy the car next year. However, with a loan of $50, he would be able both to buy the car and take a long holiday without saving at all today (although later on he will need to save to repay the debt). Japelli and Pagano (1994), among others, contribute favourable evidence to this negative relationship between saving and the financial system.[7]

In spite of the undeniable importance of the financial system in the growth process, it is no less true that companies finance their investments primarily with retained earnings. As we saw in part I, the main causes of this decision are the information problems between

---

[7] Let us highlight the fact that more saving does not necessarily mean that individuals are better off. Some people with a strong preference for consuming today may be willing to save very little and even get indebted to finance a higher level of consumption. Although this might reduce investment and growth, welfare would still be high.

Table 5.1 *Personal saving and corporate saving in the world*[a]

	Corporate saving	Personal saving	Private saving	Corporate saving	Personal saving	**Total**
	As a percentage of GDP			As a percentage of private saving		
Developed countries						
Canada	8.5	9.8	18.3	46.4	53.6	**100.0**
France	10.7	9.5	20.2	53.0	47.0	**100.0**
Germany	13.0	8.2	21.2	61.3	38.7	**100.0**
Italy	5.4	19.2	24.6	22.0	78.0	**100.0**
Japan	12.4	13.2	25.6	48.4	51.6	**100.0**
Spain	12.4	7.8	20.2	61.4	38.6	**100.0**
United Kingdom	8.0	7.1	15.1	53.0	47.0	**100.0**
United States	9.1	9.0	18.1	50.3	49.7	**100.0**
Average	9.9	10.5	20.4	49.5	50.5	**100.0**
Latin America						
Argentina	13.0	3.1	16.1	80.9	19.1	**100.0**
Brazil	11.5	4.4	16.0	72.2	27.8	**100.0**
Chile	14.6	5.9	20.6	71.1	28.9	**100.0**
Colombia	10.5	1.1	11.7	90.4	9.6	**100.0**
Venezuela	14.1	6.9	21.0	67.1	32.9	**100.0**
Average	13.7	2.6	16.3	86.4	13.6	**100.0**

Note: [a]The figures correspond to averages from 1990 to 1995 in developed countries and 1990 to 1996 in Latin America.
Source: Bebczuk (1999).

creditors and borrowers and the subsequent increase in the cost of the external funds. An implication of such a finding is that the usual portrayal of families as savers and firms as borrowers lacks practical support. In fact, firms appeal to the financial system as a last resort and in marginal magnitudes. In table 5.1 private sector saving is broken down into **personal saving** (the difference between personal income and consumption) and **corporate saving** (the difference between corporate income and dividends, that is, retained earnings).

Corporate saving represents nearly 50 per cent of private saving in developed countries and 86 per cent in Latin America. We also see that the private saving rate in developed countries (20.4 per cent of GDP) is higher than that of the Latin American countries (16.3 per cent), but corporate saving is larger in Latin America (13.7 per cent against 9.9 per cent). Of particular interest is the fact that *these figures strongly contradict the presumed flow of saving from families to firms through the financial system: in practice, to a large extent, firms save and reinvest their own saving.*

Nevertheless, this does not mean that consumer saving is independent of business saving. In fact, company shares are generally owned by consumers, and it is these consumers who decide total saving. In theory, if companies decide to save less, consumers will increase in equal magnitude their personal saving to reach the level of total saving desired in the first place. If this adjustment takes place, it is said that consumers pierce the **corporate veil**, or that they understand and counteract any change in corporate saving. In reality, this compensation is only partial. Poterba (1987) calculates for the United States that an increase of $1 in corporate saving reduces personal saving by $0.50–$0.75. Bebczuk (1999) finds this contraction for Latin America to be around $0.60.

Why does total saving fall when, for example, dividends increase (namely, corporate saving falls)? Information problems that infect the credit market are once again partially responsible. For example, if consumers suffer financial constraints, they will use their dividends to increase consumption rather than save, thereby impeding full compensation. Similarly, if consumers interpret the increase of dividends as a signal of future earnings growth, they will feel wealthier and save less.

The costs and informational barriers present in the intermediation process reflect themselves in a very low level of saving intermediation. Although the financial system continues to grow swiftly, as much in size as in the volume of transactions, the heavy reliance on internal funds is a pattern that has not been much altered since the 1970s. In spite of the extraordinary development of the US financial system, retained earnings have been a more important source of funds in the last twenty-five years than they were in the previous fifty years. On the other hand, the expansion in the volume of financial transactions does not have a direct correlation with long-term corporate financing, since most transactions are short term or simply transactions in the secondary market (sale and purchase of already issued securities). For example, the volume of transactions in the forty-one main world stock markets grew at an average annual rate of 102 per cent between 1986 and 1993, but the actual number of public companies – a good indicator of access to stock financing – hardly increased by 5 per cent a year.

The subsidiary role of financial markets responds to a low supply of and a low demand for loanable funds. The *supply* is the saving that individuals decide to hand over to the financial system. Because of insoluable information problems, these individuals may be reluctant to relinquish their money, preferring instead to consume more or to invest in durable goods and real estate. The *demand* for funds by companies is also low, in this case because of the high cost of external funds as a result of intermediation costs – which decline as the financial system grows – and information problems – which are more persistent.

5.5   Resource allocation and financial fragility

A topic complementary to the previous one and that is based on the notions already considered is that of **financial fragility**. A financially fragile environment is one where individuals and firms may be seriously affected when the general financial conditions vary. In a context similar to that just described, given the prevailing informational asymmetry in financial markets, two unfavourable conditions for a country's growth can be expected:

(Claim 1) Highly profitable projects may be passed up
(Claim 2) Moderate changes in the interest rate can severely alter the operation of credit markets.

Table 5.2 *Asymmetric information and the efficiency of the financial system: a numerical example*

	Project H	Project L
EV	160	144
CF_s	200	180
CF_f	0	0
α_s	0.8	0.8
α_f	0.2	0.2
I	100	100
R	0.1	0.1
p_s	0.5	0.5
p_f	0.5	0.5
IF	0	40
C	0	30

As we have said before, leaving aside government activity, society's total income – its GDP – is simply the sum of the cash flows of all projects developed by private entrepreneurs. These cash flows eventually become the income of entrepreneurs, consumers and financial intermediaries. If information problems inhibit the materialization of high EV projects in favour of those with smaller EV, or they amplify the difficulties of financing the best projects, optimal production will not be attained.

In a world without transaction or information costs, every project whose EV exceeds the required return will be launched. Given the acceptance rule (or participation restriction) $EV \geq (1 + r)I$, those projects that maximize the private entrepreneur's benefit are precisely those that maximize society's benefit as a whole. In a world with asymmetric information (the real world), to have a project with high EV is not a sufficient condition for finding third-party financing, and entrepreneurs with risky or unproductive with more internal funds or collateral will have privileged access to external funds.

To be more explicit, let us examine the problem of a company with limited collateral needing debt to supplement its internal funds:

$$E\pi = \alpha_s[CF_s - (1 + r_L)(I - IF)] - \alpha_f C - (1 + r)IF$$
$$= \alpha_s \overline{CF}_s - \left[\frac{(1 + r)(I - IF) - p_f C}{p_s} \right] - \alpha_f C - (1 + r)IF$$

This formula should be familiar from chapter 2, the only modification being that we now permit collateral and personal funds to coexist. Knowing that both internal funds as well as collateral reduce the information premium, it is no longer obvious that projects with higher $EV = \alpha_s CF_s$ will always be selected. Let us look at a numerical example with two projects H and L subject to adverse selection and with $EV_H > EV_L$ (table 5.2).

The crucial difference between the two projects is that $EV_H > EV_L$, which makes it socially optimal from a growth point of view to undertake type H projects, but on the other hand, type L projects possess internal funds IF and collateral C.[8] The expected return, calculated from the previous formula, gives the following values:

$$E\pi_h = -\$16$$

$$E\pi_l = \$12.4$$

The situation illustrates the paradox that the entrepreneur of project H has a higher repayment risk and is thus charged a higher interest rate. The apparent inefficiency in the allocation of resources is obvious on noticing that the availability of internal funds and collateral has nothing to do with productivity. The social cost will be the $16 ($160 − $144 = $16) that society loses because the financial system finds the less productive project more attractive.[9] If type H entrepreneurs had $40 of internal funds and $30 of collateral like the entrepreneur of project L, the profit for the former would go up to $28.4, re-establishing efficiency: the difference in profit in favour of project H ($28.4 − $12.4 = $16) is equal to the difference in expected value ($160 − $144 = $16).

Having proved Claim (1), we turn to Claim (2). Let us suppose that r goes from 10 per cent to 15 per cent and that, as an unavoidable by-product, the weighted probability of success falls from 50 per cent to 40 per cent. The reader can check that, under these new conditions, project L would suffer an expected loss of −$10. It is highly probable that the only projects that are chosen to participate in the credit market are those of highly speculative nature $[EV < (1+r)I]$. Consequently, credit rationing takes place and the credit market collapses. The lesson to draw from this section is that asymmetric information makes the spontaneous operation of the credit market inefficient.

Given this market failure, state intervention could improve resource allocation. One possible mechanism is the creation of a **state guarantee system** that takes over the repayment of the debt with public funds in case the private borrower is unable to service the debt. This system eliminates the unjust disadvantage of the entrepreneur who is without asset collateral, but if access is open to any project – which will happen if the government also suffers from limited information – speculative projects are encouraged. We return to the previous example to verify this statement. To simplify, we suppose that the three projects in search of financing are H, L and T (table 5.3).

The reader can verify that the only project with a positive expected return is L (the values of the three projects are −$16, $12.4 and −$6, respectively). Having established a guarantee system for projects H and T (L projects are profitable without the guarantee), these debts will be risk-free with an interest rate of 10 per cent. As the government is in charge of the expected cost of collateral $[(1 + r)I \times \alpha_f]$ and the cost of the low loan, projects H and T become profitable for private entrepreneurs. If we want to evaluate the net profit, we should compare the derived social benefit of these projects with the cost incurred by the government, as shown in table 5.4.

If the government could discriminate among the applicants for collateral, it is evident that the subsidy for project H would be socially acceptable. But as we suppose that the

---

[8] It is assumed that there are also other types of projects in the marketplace, as implied by the fact that $\alpha_s > p_s$.
[9] We deliberately assume that both projects are equally risky, so there is no trade off between productivity and risk, which may be a negative feature of growth when individuals are risk averse.

Table 5.3 *The effects of a state guarantee*
system: a numerical example

	Project H	Project L	Project T
EV	160	144	60
CF_s	200	180	200
CF_f	0	0	0
α_s	0.8	0.8	0.3
α_f	0.2	0.2	0.7
I	100	100	100
r	0.1	0.1	0.1
p_s	0.5	0.5	0.5
p_f	0.5	0.5	0.5
IF	0	40	0
C	0	30	0

Table 5.4 *Net social benefit of a state guarantee*
system

	Project H	Project T
EV	160	60
$(1 + r)I$	110	110
Social benefit	50	−50
Social cost	22	77
$[(1 + r)I \times \alpha_f]$		
Net social benefit	**28**	**−127**

government agency lacks the necessary information, project T will also be approved, not only generating an obligation for the system but also a negative net social benefit. In the example, the guarantee system is inefficient with a net social cost of $99 ($28 − $127 = $99). Naturally, we cannot assert that this will always be the result, since it will depend on the characteristics of potential projects and of the government's ability to select the most profitable ventures. It is necessary to highlight that credit support for small companies, the usual victims of information problems, exists in both developed and developing countries, but that they cover a small fraction of total loans.

5.6   Legal structure and the development of capital markets

In the past few years, a new and promising line of investigation that links the development of the financial system with the **legal structure** of a country via information problems has emerged. The core of this approach is that **corporate governance** – the rules under which the firm relates to its financial stakeholders (creditors and shareholders), and how all of them deal with their mutual conflicts of interests – is crucial when determining the willingness of outside investors to provide funding.

Since creditors are outsiders to the firm who lack any direct power over the decision-making process, **creditor rights** must be properly protected from adverse selection and moral hazard on the part of borrowers. Let us suppose that a company that has fully guaranteed its loan makes insufficient revenue to repay its debt. In country 1, where the laws are decidedly pro-lender, the transfer of collateral is achieved quickly and at a reasonably low cost. In country 2, by contrast, the bankruptcy process is slow and expensive, the incumbent managers are not removed from the company in financial distress, they have the legal freedom to unload assets and pay extraordinary dividends and not even secured lenders are paid with certainty. What should we expect to happen in these different countries? Poor legal protection forces lenders to cover themselves by means of a higher interest rate, lending short term, and sometimes rationing the supply of capital. The protection that comes from the law acts as a substitute, although incomplete, for the lack of information and control that creditors suffer. In this way the legal framework conditions the willingness of savers to finance third-party projects.[10]

La Porta *et al.* (1997) gathered information for different representative indicators of the legal structure for forty-nine countries, elaborating an index of creditor rights. This index, based on the analysis of company and commercial laws, ranges between 0 and 4. A particular finding of the study is that marked differences exist among countries according to the historical origin of the legal structure. Four large legal systems can be categorised – English, French, German and Scandinavian – with the English classified as the most favourable and the French as the least favourable to the interests of lenders. Consistent with our discussion above, countries in the English tradition have on average the most developed financial systems (measured by private debt over GDP) and those of French tradition the least developed (table 5.5).

The econometric results also lend support to this hypothesis. An indicator of the quality and efficiency of the judicial system, or *rule of law*, which assesses how well the legal framework is actually implemented, also appears as a fundamental determinant of financial development. Clearly, if the actual enforcement of bankruptcy laws is lax, even the best-designed legal body will most likely fail, as experience in many developing countries demonstrates.

An issue ignored up to now is the protection of **shareholder rights**. As an insider to the firm, the manager can pursue deceitful actions at the expense of shareholders, as shown in chapter 3. Although the board of directors is designed to work in favour of shareholders' interests, it is also true that this might not always be the case, especially when managers possess equity or have special arrangements with board members. In the end, the lack of disclosure and power over the firm may turn investors away from stock markets. While in

---

[10] A sensitive issue because of its social effects on employment and production is for the courts and stakeholders to wisely decide whether the firm deserves a second chance keeping it a going concern (*rehabilitation*) or is just a lost cause and thus the best strategy is for the firm to cease its activity selling its assets for salvage value (*liquidation*). When liquidation is socially convenient, strong creditor rights are the way to go. But if the firm is viable in the medium and long run, such protection to lenders may prevent the firm from continuing and recovering.

Table 5.5 *Legal origin and financial development*

Legal origin	Index of creditor rights	Private debt over GDP
English	3.11	0.68
French	1.58	0.45
Latin America	1.25	0.29
German	2.33	0.97
Scandinavian	2.00	0.57

Source: La Porta *et al.* (1997).

theory shareholders own the firm and have some decision power proportional to their equity package, most of them are in practice outsiders.

In particular, **minority shareholders** may find it much less appealing to exert their statutory rights, collect information and monitor the firm than large shareholders, namely, those with about 10 per cent of total equity or more. The main control mechanism in the hands of minority shareholders is the right to vote for the board of directors and also on important corporate decisions such as mergers and acquisitions. However, voting rights may be costly to exercise. For example, voting by mail may be not permitted, requiring the shareholder to attend the meeting. In some other cases, managers do not provide shareholders with enough information on the voting process, discouraging their participation in the firm's matters. La Porta *et al.* (1997) produced an index of minority shareholders' rights, finding that English legal origin countries again rank first, followed by Scandinavian countries, and with French and German countries showing the poorest indexes. Schleifer and Vishny (1997) review the literature on corporate governance, and present compelling cases and evidence on the lack of protection that minority shareholders suffer.

5.7   The quantitative importance of the financial system for the rate of economic growth

We shall show here that the theoretical connection between financial development and *per capita* economic growth is supported by the empirical evidence. We shall also document the negative effect of information problems in financial markets on growth. In the appendix to the chapter (p. 92) we will briefly review the foundation of econometrics, the statistical method used in economics.

An abundant literature has convincingly proved that the financial system exerts a significant influence on the economic growth of countries, once other factors are controlled for, such as the initial income of the country, education level, trade openness and economic and institutional stability. These studies use different indicators of financial development, the most popular being the volume of credit to non-financial private sector companies as a percentage of GDP. In a rigorous study, Beck, Levine and Loayza (2000) find that an increase of 1 percentage point in credit to GDP ratio permanently elevates the annual growth rate about 1 percentage point when initial financial development is low.

This figure may seem too small, but it is not. Let us take Argentina as an example. In the period analysed (1960–95), the credit to GDP ratio was on average 16 per cent, while the average in all developing countries was 25 per cent. If Argentina had reached at least that value, its rate of *per capita* annual growth would have been 1.1 percentage points higher than what it actually was, an average annual 1.8 per cent. To appreciate the magnitude of this effect, it is necessary to consider the 'magic of compounded interest'. Let us suppose that *per capita* GDP is originally $100. Growing at 1.8 per cent annually, after one year it will become $101.1 ($100 × 1.018 = $101.8), after the second ($101.8 × 1.011 = $102.9), and so forth. In a longer term, say twenty years, the *per capita* GDP will have gone from $100 to $142.9 ($100 × 1.018^{20} = $142.9). Now, if Argentina had enjoyed a level of financial development similar to the developing-country average, its rate of annual growth could have been 2.9 per cent (1.8 per cent + 1.1 per cent = 2.9 per cent) and after 20 years, the *per capita* GDP would have been $177.1.

Rajan and Zingales (1998) adopted a different methodology but found similar results. Differences in the scale of projects and in their maturation time create differences among industries in the degree of dependence on external funds, measured by the difference between productive investments and operative cash flows. In this way, financial development should impel the growth of industries highly dependent on external funds. The results, based on data from more than thirty industries and countries, are auspicious; specifically, Rajan and Zingales find that an industry with high dependence would grow on average 1.3 percentage points more per year than an industry with low dependence, if it was located in a country with high rather than low financial development.

The basic challenge when trying to find an empirical nexus between financial development, information problems and economic growth is that *information problems are not directly observable*. Bebczuk (1999) nevertheless shows that the proportion of credit financing over total investment is a good proxy for asymmetric information in financial markets: the more severe the information asymmetry, the lower will be both the supply and demand for external financing. Bebczuk thus finds, with data for forty countries, that increasing this ratio (reducing information problems) can considerably accelerate growth. For Argentina, the rate of growth could increase 0.4 percentage points per year just by reaching the world's average relationship of credit over investment. This effect suggests that financial constraints halt growth, in the sense that many profitable investments are discarded because information problems prevent companies from obtaining reasonable financing costs.

Lastly, it is crucial to note that although most of our discussion revolves around bank credit, Levine and Zervos (1998) show evidence favouring a positive relationship between the development of the stock market and growth. Besides sharing the benefits described in section 5.3, the stock market has the additional advantages of providing liquidity to investors, extending the term of financing, and making available a wider menu of financial instruments for risk diversification. Risk sharing also encourages investors to support high-productivity and high-risk projects.

A related issue is whether bank-based or market-based countries are better equipped to promote long-run growth. For instance, on information grounds, market-based systems are better at encouraging information quality and disclosure *vis-à-vis* investors and disciplining managers through the informational content of securities transactions and the threat of hostile takeovers. On the other hand, banks have a relative advantage in the closer relationship they establish with borrowers. Nevertheless, Levine (2000) does not reach a conclusive empirical result in favour of a particular system: what really matters is the size of the financial system as a whole rather than its structure.

5.8   Discussion

The mere existence of the financial system is the defining indicator of the practical relevance of information problems. Based on a high degree of professionalism and responsibility, financial intermediaries are given the trust – and, more importantly, part of the savings – of the depositors of a community. Without them, communication between savers and borrowers would be chaotic and inefficient. It is not by chance that banks, as we know them today, were born in the twilight of the Middle Ages, precisely at the moment when societies began to modernize and the volume and complexity of financial transactions started to exceed the capacity of merchants, who had become rudimentary bankers.

Financial intermediaries try to reconcile at a reasonable cost the different preferences for risk and liquidity between savers and borrowers. These transaction and information costs do not however, achieve, the eradication of the problems of information that have occupied us, although they do make it less probable than an opportunist debtor will be successful.

Until the early 1990s economic growth specialists with relative unanimity, rejected, the financial system as an independent engine of growth. Adhering to the conviction that financing was irrelevant, they determined that growth was a function of the investments undertaken, not how they were financed. Consequently, financial development was a mere by-product of economic development. What these researchers failed to recognize was that the quantity and quality of investments was not independent of the origin of funds. Financial intermediaries are responsible for a socially efficient mobilization of savings, including the reduction of transaction costs as well as the selection of the most productive projects.

A substantial body of research has attempted to quantify the effect on economic growth. The overwhelming weight of internal funds demonstrates that, even with very developed financial systems, information problems have not been resolved and probably will not be in the immediate future. The consequence is that many profitable investment opportunities whose macroeconomic result is accelerated growth are not undertaken for lack of financing. These financial constraints reduce long-term growth and, as we shall see, generate undesirable fluctuations in the level of short-term activity.

Appendix: econometrics and regression, or how data should be interpreted

When considering the practical validity of a certain theory, the economist uses a branch of statistics called **econometrics**. In particular, a well-known technique known as **regression**

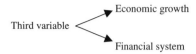

Figure 5A.1

is used to study the variation of a certain variable in terms of others that the theory has identified as explanatory. In our case, the dependent variable is the rate of growth and the independent variables are a series of economic and institutional indicators capable of influencing the volume of investment and/or technological progress.

The advantage of this technique is that it allows the researcher to analyse the combined effect of different variables and to extract the individual effect of each. It is important to consider all the variables at the same time because in failing to do so one is at risk of misinterpreting the data. In our case, it is possible that the size of the financial system moves in the same direction as the rate of growth, from which we could conclude that the financial system elevates the rate of growth:

$$\text{Financial system} \to \text{Economic growth}$$

This is just an initial hypothesis. It may be true, but such a positive association could be due to two very different explanations. On the one hand, growth can induce the development of the financial system, instead of the reverse:

$$\text{Economic growth} \to \text{Financial system}$$

When the country grows, the volume of deposits grows and, given economies of scale, financial transactions become less expensive, expanding the financial system. On the other hand, the positive correlation could appear because a third variable influences both at the same time, causing movement in unison (figure 5A.1).

This situation would happen if, for example, the population desired to increase saving. On Through greater saving, investment would rise and the rate of growth would increase. Simultaneously, the increase in saving would create more deposits and an expansion of the financial system.

In synthesis, the correlation between two variables can be deceptive, and decisions based on it can be completely ineffective. In our case, if the correlation was due to the presence of a third variable, a policy of growth founded on the expansion of the financial system would be useless, since it is saving that should be stimulated. Econometric techniques try to perfect this type of quantitative analysis in order to avoid these mistakes, employing sophisticated knowledge of statistics. A good introduction is Gujarati (1990).

Another precaution in order to derive robust conclusions is to make sure that the sample size of analysed cases is as extensive as possible. Individual data is a good starting point to begin with, but we are not allowed to claim that the discovery is applicable to other countries or periods. Also, it is vital that the researcher does not manipulate the data by discarding those cases that are not supportive of his theory.

For example, it should not be claimed that the financial system promotes growth just because in the past two years growth was quicker at the same time that credit volume grew. This could be a coincidence that may not continue. In our case, a good part of the evidence covers a thirty-five-year period (1960–95) for more than 100 countries.

Lack of care allows one to infer absurd conclusions. For example, we could assert that watching television promotes economic growth. After all, starting from 1945, television has exploded in popularity as people spend more time in front of screens, while at the same time the world is witnessing incredible growth. If we constructed a graph we would see that the development of television and economic growth have moved in the same direction. This statistical truth constitutes an economic fallacy. Correct reasoning would be that economic growth, increasing income and diminishing the length of a day's labour, has driven the popularity of television. Even so, this explanation would only be partial, since we would be omitting the technological factor that made the invention possible and led to the small screen (which would not have been so small without the technological factor). We could keep going, wondering if these technological advances might not be explained by the expanded demand created by revenue growth.

We will stop here to avoid being confusing, but the conclusion should be evident: to 'give voice' to data is not difficult, but to make them 'tell the truth' is. The other latent danger is that a researcher who begins with preconceived notions can torture data until she finds the desired explanation.

An example of coincidence without causation both real and amusing is the market prediction for the championship of American Football in the United States. The final confrontation pits one team from the National Football Conference (NFC) and one from the American Football Conference (AFC) to settle the winner of the coveted trophy, the Super Bowl. It has been found that, throughout twenty years and with rare exceptions, the stock market rises every time a team from the NFC wins and falls if the winner comes from the AFC. Although the correlation is attractive, there is no economic argument that sustains it, so that it does not merit any investigation. In any event, the number of observations is not considerable enough, and we should expect that as more and more championships and years go by, the correlation will disappear.

To sum up, serious empirical evidence requires (a) a convincing theory; (b) an extensive number of cases chosen at random; (c) a regression analysis and other statistical tests. As it is possible to use different methods and econometric techniques, this formula is not infallible and it is not unheard of for two researchers to come to opposite conclusions by varying the sample data or the methodology employed.

An exception to these rules is what are called *natural experiments*: when an unforeseen disruption in the economic conditions takes place, it can be illuminating to study the circumstances before and after to measure the particular effect of the triggering variable. Examples of this are the unexpected oil crisis of 1973 and the debt crisis in 1982, which have served as opportunities to study company and country behaviour before the sudden explosion of these incidents. Also within this sphere are the *case studies* that are widely popular in the field of finance. In these, the reaction of markets to corporate announcements (mergers, a change in dividend policy, a bond issue, etc.) are studied, analysing stock returns before and after word gets out.

In these situations, the sample size of cases can be small and it may not be necessary to consider other variables apart from what provokes the study. The reason for this procedure is that the change in the variable of interest is so unexpected and abrupt that it can be safely assumed to be totally independent of other variables, offering the windfall of a 'laboratory experiment' in which all environmental conditions are controlled. The economy, in its role as social science, does not have control over the turbulent social context in which many relevant factors change at the same time. The economist is a passive observer of reality, not a creator of experiments (assuming no political or ministerial power). Gathering data on many cases and keeping in mind how other variables that influence the issue have behaved are forms of rectifying this deficiency.

Bibliography

Bebczuk, R. (1999), *Essays in Corporate Saving, Financial Development, and Growth*, unpublished doctoral thesis, University of Illinois at Urbana-Champaign.
  Cited in chapter 1; chapter 1 discusses and estimates the effect of information asymmetry on economic growth in forty countries, while chapter 2 presents calculations of personal and business saving in different countries and discusses the implications of the 'corporate veil'.
  (2000), 'Guidelines for an efficient state guarantee system for SMEs loans', Working Paper, Department of Economics, Universidad Nacional de La Plata.
  This presents the basic elements to be taken into account when designing a state guarantee programme.
Beck, T., Levine, R. and Loayza, N. (2000). 'Finance and the sources of growth', *Journal of Financial Economics*, 58(1).
Demirgüç-Kunt, A. and R. Levine (1996), 'Stock market development and financial intermediaries: stylized facts', *World Bank Economic Review*, 10(2), 291–321.
  A comparative study of forty-four countries on stock market development and bank and non-bank debt.
Demirgüç-Kunt, A. and V. Maksimovic (1996), 'Stock market development and financing choices of firms', *World Bank Economic Review*, 10(2), 341–69.
  An extensive study of the relationship between company financing decisions and national financial evolution for thirty developed and developing countries.
Gujárati, D. (1990), *Econometrics*, Bogotá: McGraw-Hill.
Japelli, T. and M. Pagano (1994), 'Saving, growth, and liquidity constraints', *Quarterly Journal of Economics*, 109(1)83–109.
  A formal and empirical study on the effect of liquidity restrictions on saving and growth.
LaPorta, R., F. López de Silanes, A. Shleifer and R. Vishny (1997), 'Legal determinants of external finance', *Journal of Finance*, 52(3), 1131–50.
  Through different quantitative and qualitative measures of judicial classification and legal protection for creditors and shareholders, this finds persuasive international evidence that such measures positively influence the development of the credit market.
Levine R. (1997), 'Financial development and economic growth: views and agenda', *Journal of Economic Literature*, 35.
  A revision of the channels through which financial development is transferred to growth; it includes successive studies on the topic.
Levine, R. (2000), 'Market-based or bank-based financial systems: which is better?', University of Minnesota, mimeo.
  An empirical investigation shedding some light on the relative merits of both systems.

Levine, R., N. Loayza and T. Beck (1999), 'Financial intermediation and growth: causality and causes', *Journal of Financial Economics*.

This includes recent and robust evidence for financial development causing growth for a wide sample of countries.

Levine, R. and S. Zervos (1998), 'Stock markets and economic growth', *American Economic Growth*, 88(3), 537–58.

This explores the association between the development of the stock market and growth, finding a positive relationship.

Oliner, S. and G. Rudebusch (1992), 'Sources of the financing hierarchy for business investment', *Review of Economics and Statistics*, 74, 643–54.

One of the few studies that tries to measure the importance of information and agency problems for corporate financing against the alternative approach based on transaction costs.

Poterba, J. (1987), 'Tax policy and corporate saving', *Brookings Papers on Economic Activity*, 2, 455–503.

One of the rare works that empirically analyses the nexus between personal and business saving, using data from the United States.

Rajan, R. and L. Zingales (1998), 'Financial dependence and growth', *American Economic Review*, 88(3), 559–86.

Presents and applies an original methodology for evaluating the relevance of financial development on economic growth.

Shleifer, A. and Vishny (1997), 'A survey of corporate governance', *Journal of Finance*, 52, 737–83.

An excellent review of the theory and evidence on the conflicts of interest among the various firm stakeholders.

6 Asymmetric information and business cycles

Business cycles are as frequent as they are undesirable. Consumption and, to a greater extent investment, changes considerably from one quarter to the next, affecting welfare as well as the necessary predictability that business demands.

There is little doubt that these are good enough reasons to stimulate research interest in the topic. Much effort has been devoted to understanding the origins of economic recessions and booms, but for a long time researchers have lacked a solid explanation for the duration and depth of the fluctuations that follow small initial shocks. Asymmetric information theory has made a substantial contribution to the matter, illuminating the role played by financial factors in the economy's short-term dynamics.

Building on the notions introduced in chapter 3, we shall see how a recession materializes and spreads. The differential cost of financing sources renders the availability of internal funds and collateral a crucial variable for understanding output fluctuations. The issue at hand can displayed in the graph in figure 6.1. The thick line shows the evolution of GDP over time in the face a negative shock (the vertical drop in GDP) in the absence of financial factors, while the dotted line reflects the amplifying influence of asymmetric information problems in financial markets, which end up deepening and prolonging the effect of the original shock.[1]

6.1 Corporate investment and internal funds

How does a company choose its investments? As a first step, the entrepreneur calculates each project's expected cash flow. Next, she determines the corresponding cost of capital cc, and then chooses those yielding the highest profit. Let us imagine a company that can take on three possible projects, classified in descending order of expected value, H, M and L. They all require an initial investment I, which involves a certain cost of capital. Additional projects do not even recover the invested capital. The company will accept all the projects with a positive expected profit, but should know the corresponding cost of capital upon making that decision. To give form to this plan, let us assume that the projects have the

---

[1] This negative shock can take different forms: a higher international interest rate, a slower demand for exports, an episode of political or social unrest, or a reduced level of consumption due to more pessimistic expectations.

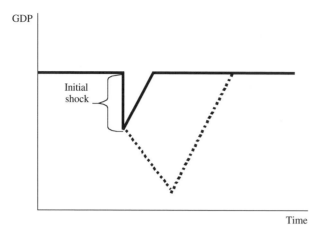

Figure 6.1 Recessions under asymmetric information

following expected values: $EV_h = \$135$, $EV_m = \$125$ and $EV_l = \$115$ and three possible costs of capital exist: 30 per cent, 20 per cent and 10 per cent. The expected profit for any one of these projects, $i = H, M$ or L, is:

$$E\pi_i = EV_i - (1 + cc)I$$

Let us calculate the three projects' expected profit as the cost of capital decreases. At 30 per cent, the projects H, M and L will offer the following expected profit:

$$E\pi_h = \$135 - 1.3 \times \$100 = \$5$$
$$E\pi_m = \$125 - 1.3 \times \$100 = -\$5$$
$$E\pi_l = \$115 - 1.3 \times \$100 = -\$15$$

Repeating the same exercise with a 20 per cent cost of capital we find that:

$$E\pi_h = \$135 - 1.2 \times \$100 = \$15$$
$$E\pi_m = \$125 - 1.2 \times \$100 = \$5$$
$$E\pi_l = \$115 - 1.2 \times \$100 = -\$5$$

while at 10 per cent we have:

$$E\pi_h = \$135 - 1.1 \times \$100 = \$25$$
$$E\pi_m = \$125 - 1.1 \times \$100 = \$15$$
$$E\pi_l = \$115 - 1.1 \times \$100 = \$5$$

Next, the entrepreneur will put together a table identifying the acceptable projects at each possible cost of capital (table 6.1).

Table 6.1 represents the company's investment demand. It tells us something completely intuitive: the demand for investment increases as the cost of capital falls – as in the case of any good or service, the lower the price, the higher the demand. The graph in figure 6.2 will help us see the idea.

Table 6.1 *Acceptable projects*

Cost of capital (%)	Acceptable projects (positive $E\pi$)	Total investment ($)
30	H	100
20	H, M	200
10	H, M, L	300

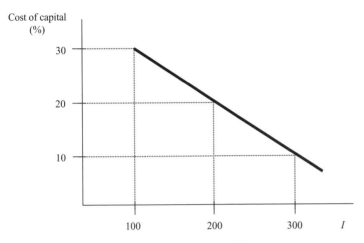

Figure 6.2   Investment demand and cost of capital

The negative slope of the demand curve is a consequence of the **diminishing marginal productivity** of capital. In this context 'marginal' means additional, and captures the notion that investment opportunities are eventually exhausted as more projects are undertaken.

As in all markets that are determined by price, it is necessary simultaneously to consider the supply and demand. The investment demand is a *demand for loanable funds*. The *supply of loanable funds* includes both internal funds and external funds (bank credit, stocks and bonds). As became clear in chapters 2 and 3, the opportunity cost of internal funds equals the required return. Assuming that the required return is 10 per cent and that the entrepreneur has enough internal funds to finance any level of investment, the supply of loanable funds would be a horizontal line at 10 per cent (figure 6.3).

The desired investment level is defined by the intersection of the supply and demand schedules (figure 6.4).

When $I = \$300$, the supply and demand of funds is equal. This value represents an equilibrium: if the company invested less, it would lose $5, the expected profit of project L financed at 10 per cent. If it invested more, it would directly lose money as additional projects have negative net present value (NPV).

How would the analysis be modified under asymmetric information? From section 3.3 we know that stock financing is more expensive than debt, which in turn is more costly

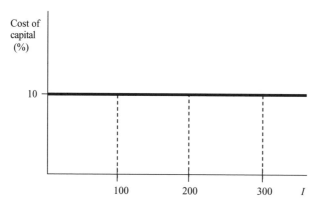

Figure 6.3   Supply of loanable funds

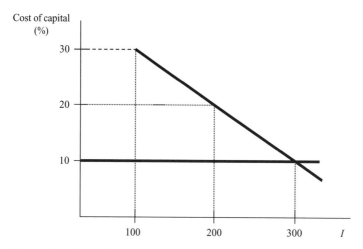

Figure 6.4   Desired investment level

than retained earnings. The motivating dilemma of this section is that the unavailability of internal funds can impede carrying out all the profitable investments. Let us suppose that the internal funds' opportunity cost is still 10 per cent, but the entrepreneur pays 20 per cent on debt and 30 per cent on stock. Let us suppose that the entrepreneur possesses only $100 of retained earnings, and has access to $100 of debt and $100 of stock. The supply and demand graph for this situation is shown in figure 6.5.

Now the supply of funds is no longer a horizontal line at 10 per cent, as the cost of funds begins to grow once the company resorts to external financing. Project *H* can be financed at 10 per cent with internal funds and project *M* at 20 per cent with debt, but project *L* should be funded by stock at 30 per cent, which would lead to the project to be passed up since it yields a $15 loss. As a result, the company will invest only $200 instead of the $300 that it would have if information problems did not exist. This **investment–cash flow sensitivity**, namely the pronounced impact of the availability of internal funds on

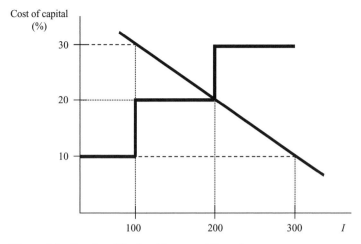

Figure 6.5   Supply of funds with external financing

investment, has driven an active research programme since the mid-1980s. These studies have successfully demonstrated that, given their respective investment opportunities, firms that have more internal funds invest more.

This outcome is a corollary of the failure of the Modigliani–Miller theorem, which we discussed in chapter 3. On practical grounds, financial issues do matter, as a firm having enough internal funds will face a smaller cost of capital and thus will be able to invest and earn more than another company with a greater dependence on external funds. We shall call **information premium**, IP, the gap between the effective cost of capital and the cost of internal funds: $IP = cc - r$.

When faced with information problems, investment decisions are no longer independent of financing decisions.[2] Now, although the entrepreneur has good investment opportunities, some of them cannot be exploited because of the lack of financing – a firm in this situation is said to suffer a **financial constraint**.

The financing 'escalator' leaves us with the uncomfortable impression that the cost of capital increases abruptly, passing, for example, from 10 per cent to 20 per cent when the investment goes from $199 to $201. For our purposes, a nicer representation of the supply of funds is the graph in figure 6.6.

One way to understand figure 6.6 is to accept that, with the exhaustion of internal funds, a company will resort to secured debt (in a bad event, posted collateral fully covers both principal and the risk-free interest rate). Remember that secured debt has the same cost as internal funds. Given the availability of internal funds and collateral, the portion of non-secured debt and the corresponding cost of capital will increase with the total amount of investment as a consequence of information problems. We shall come back to this point in section 6.4.

---

[2] The independence between the investment and financing decisions in perfect capital markets is known as **Fisher's Separation Theorem**, in honour of the American economist Irving Fisher.

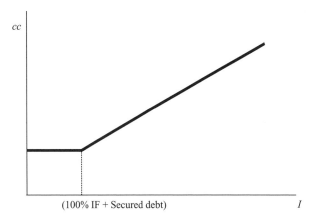

cc

(100% IF + Secured debt)   *I*

Figure 6.6 A smoother supply curve

6.2 Evidence on financial constraints and cash flow sensitivity

How important is cash flow sensitivity in the real world? We shall show in this section that, if we ignore financial factors, we shall make serious mistakes when predicting the level of entrepreneurial investment. But before we present these numbers, it is useful to describe the procedure that researchers follow to detect this cash flow sensitivity.

The main empirical challenge is that researchers cannot observe all the company's investment opportunities but rather only those that are taken on and are included in the company's financial statements. However, some publicly available information can be used to understand how the company makes its investment decisions. If the capital markets function correctly, the market value in the stock exchange reflects the company's expected future profits. At the same time, its financial statements record the current market value of assets. Consequently, the **market-to-book ratio** is an appropriate measure of the incentive to invest: if the ratio is larger than 1, the benefits exceed costs and the company will find the investment profitable.

This variable is used frequently in the stock market to evaluate the quality of company stock prices. The origin of the widespread use of this concept goes back to an economic theory article written in 1969 by James Tobin who, as we saw earlier, went on to receive the Nobel Prize in 1981 for his many contributions to the economic science. (Many market operators that think about the irrelevance of economic theory will appreciate the irony.) Subsequent papers started naming this ratio as **Tobin's *q***, *q* being the symbol which Tobin used to denominate the ratio.[3]

In a perfect financial market, all that is needed to predict a company's investment is to know their *q*, as the firm will undertake all projects with *q* equal or greater than 1, using either internal or external funds. But, as we have just learned, under asymmetric information

---

[3] An insolvable problem with the calculation of Tobin's *q* is that it is not based on the incremental (*marginal*) benefits and costs of an additional investment, but on the benefits and costs from the whole stock of capital of the firm, which will not necessarily coincide with the former. Anyway, under certain conditions, the marginal and the average *q* have the same value.

some profitable projects may be passed up if the firm has scarce internal funds. Using our previous notation, q can be defined as:

$$q = \frac{P}{I}$$
$$= \frac{EV}{(1+r)I}$$

Note that the expected value of each project is discounted at the required rate of return. In this sense, q is a 'pure' measure of the profitability of a project, calculated in a Modigliani–Miller world and thus free from information problems. For the example that we are assessing, q assumes the following values:

$$q_h = \frac{\$13.5}{1.1 \times \$100} = 1.227$$

$$q_m = \frac{\$125}{1.1 \times \$100} = 1.136$$

$$q_1 = \frac{\$135}{1.1 \times \$100} = 1.045$$

It should not be surprising that q produces the same ranking of projects as the expected profit does. It is evident that the three projects would be taken on if the cost of capital cc were equal to the required return r, which would happen if the credit market were free of imperfections.

All these concepts are used by researchers intending to examine the relevance of financial constraints in the real world. If investment is responsive not only to q but also to cash flows (internal funds), we have an indication that financial constraints do exist – firms without sufficient own funds invest less because external funds are more expensive. In other words, internal funds represent a *proxy* variable of the asymmetric information problems, which are *not directly observable*.

We can see the effect of a change in internal funds on investment in figure 6.7.[4]

After an increase in internal funds from IF_0 to IF_1, the information premium is smaller at each possible investment level, which turns projects that were unprofitable at the initial cost of capital into profitable ventures. The investment goes from I_0 to I_1, and this increment is not a result of new and valuable investment opportunities (which would have shifted the investment demand function to the right) but merely of more favourable financial conditions. The lesson is clear: *when there is asymmetric information, investment and financing decisions are no longer independent.*

Empirical studies along these lines tend to support the presumption that firms prone to suffer financial constraints depend significantly on internal funds.[5] The next question is how widespread the problem is. For example, if most firms with public offerings are subjected to financial constraints, that would mean that other firms, which are surely more exposed

---

[4] For simplicity, we are assuming that the firm has no collateral.
[5] Small and young firms, those that belong to financial or industrial groups, those that have issued stock or debt in the past, and those without a risk rating from a reputable agency, among other characteristics, are more likely to face financial constraints.

Table 6.2 *Estimated effect of cash flow and q on investment, public companies in selected countries*

	Cash flow[a]	Cash stock[b]	q^c
United States	0.181	0.062	0.057
Canada	0.463	0.084	0.047
France	0.308	0.020	0.038
Germany	0.482	0.063	0.035
Great Britain	0.706	0.075	0.035
Japan	0.217	0.037	0.029

Note: [a]Cash flow: Net earnings + depreciation, amortized intangibles and deferred taxes.
[b]Cash stock: Cash + liquid investments.
[c]q: (Market value of common shares + book value of preferred stock + book value of the debt)/(Book value of the company).
Source: Kadapakkam, Kumar and Riddick (1998).

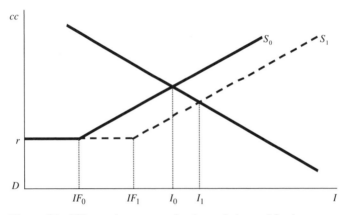

Figure 6.7   Effect on investment of a change in internal funds

to asymmetric information problems, experience even more severe constraints. From here, we can predict that the problem has macroeconomic implications. Table 6.2 shows the investment – cash flow sensitivity for public firms in developed countries.[6]

The effect of internal funds is captured in table 6.2 by two variables: *Cash flow*, which measures the cash generated by the company during the year, and *Cash stock*, the cash and liquid investments accumulated from previous years. Since we shall soon return to

---

[6] These results come from a regression with panel data for the period 1982–91 for each one of the countries. The number of observations varies from 534 (Japan) to 13,547 (United States). Variables are expressed as a proportion of the net fixed assets; besides these variables, the regression includes sales. All the explanatory variables correspond to the previous period. All the coefficients that appear in table 6.2 are statistically significant at 5 per cent.

this table, we shall say only that the internal funds sensitivity seems to be significant, in sharp contrast to macroeconomic analysis that tends to underestimate or ignore the role of information problems when predicting private investment. For comparative reasons, it is worth noting that a recent study for Latin American countries finds an investment–internal funds sensitivity of 0.762 for all companies (with or without public offering).[7] The noticeable impact of cash flows in both country groups points to the conclusion that *information problems are a natural flaw in the operation of all economies and not only of less developed ones.*

6.3 Business cycles and the financial accelerator

An observation that has intrigued macroeconomic analysts for years is that *marginal changes in economic conditions cause pronounced changes in the level of economic activity.* For example, it has been found that small and temporary increases in the interest rate cause long-lasting recessions. Other interesting cases are the oil crises of 1973 and 1979, where a small increase in production costs was associated with severe recessions.

Again, the research on asymmetric information in financial markets opened new horizons in the debate. A simple extension of the corporate financing issues dealt with in chapter 3 and in previous sections of this chapter will allow us to explain this intriguing phenomenon. This branch of analysis has been called the **financial accelerator**. The idea is that when an unfavourable event hits a company – for example, an increase in the interest rate, a fall in sales or an increase in production costs – there is, beyond the direct impact on its earnings, an additional effect in the loss of retained earnings and in the value of assets. On decreasing the self-financing capacity and the value of potential credit guarantees, not only the necessity of external financing grows but also its cost. In other words, financial constraints *accelerate* the ongoing recession.

We shall proceed by first introducing the operation of the financial accelerator when the origin of the recession is a *real* phenomenon, caused by the production process, such as a fall in sales or an increase in operating costs. The consequent decline of internal funds is depicted in figure 6.7. The difference with the financial accelerator after a *monetary* shock is subtle yet decisive. We shall expand on monetary policy in the next section. Figure 6.8 is a roadmap for the rest of the chapter.

As a recession has two dimensions (its immediate effect and its effects over time) we need to be precise in distinguishing them. Chronologically, we can describe the process at work as in figure 6.9.

First of all, at what we call time t_0, the company generates from its ongoing projects, internal funds that will serve to finance either partially or totally its new projects. After investing at time t_1, the company collects the cash flow at time t_2.

---

[7] See Bebczuk (1999). The methodology in this case is different from the one explained in the text and thus not strictly comparable with the previous coefficients. In particular, the regression with panel data from 1990–96 is based on aggregate series on domestic and international sources of funding of non-financial firms. Countries included are Argentina, Brazil, Chile, Colombia, Mexico, Peru and Venezuela.

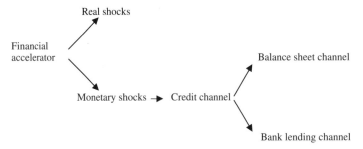

Figure 6.8 The operation of the financial accelerator

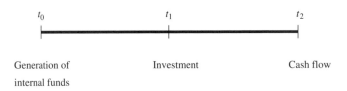

| Generation of | Investment | Cash flow |

Generation of internal funds

Figure 6.9 The cash flow cycle

We shall continue with the example developed in section 6.1 to illustrate the operation of the financial accelerator. Suppose that the company has retained earnings of $300, which would allow it to take on the three projects, H, M and L. However, an unexpected fall in sales reduces its total earnings by $100 and its internal funds to $200. If information problems did not exist and other changes do not take place in the economy, the company could still invest $300 by resorting to, say, a bank loan at 10 per cent. In this case, the level of economic activity would feel the effect of $100 at t_0 because, to make this loan effective, it is necessary that consumers spend $100 less and invest this saving in the project through the financial system. The downturn does not affect the economy only at t_0, but also at t_1, when the expected cash flow will be $375 ($135 + $125 + $115 = $375) given that all three projects are undertaken.

In presence of information flaws the effect does not stop there. With $200 of internal funds and an interest rate of 20 per cent, the entrepreneur will decide to move forward with projects H and M and will discard project L, which becomes unattractive at the new cost of capital. The economy loses $100 of investment at time t_0 and $115 of income at t_1. Now the recession is prolonged and is magnified once it reduces income at t_1 to $260 ($135 + $125 = $260). This last effect is the financial accelerator. Table 6.3 summarises the situation.

Although we have concentrated on cash flow fluctuations, the variation in the value of collateral also affects the magnitude of the financial accelerator. Financial and physical assets (property and machinery) usually serve as a guarantee. The value of these assets increases with their promised cash flows and decreases with the level of interest rates. As a result, collateral will probably be less valuable when economic growth is slow and interest rates are higher. Accordingly, the final effect would be similar to a cut in cash flows.

Table 6.3 *The financial accelerator at work*

	Internal funds t_0	Investment t_1	Expected cash flow t_2
Initial condition	300	300	375
Negative shock without asymmetric information	200	300	375
Negative shock with asymmetric information	200	200	260

6.4   Monetary policy and the credit channel

Changes in monetary policy, such as variations in interest rates or in the quantity of money, may also put the financial accelerator in motion. Central banks usually decide to raise interest rates or to reduce the quantity of money in circulation when they foresee an inflationary period, for in this manner investment and possibly consumption are discouraged. This decrease in spending or **aggregate demand**, for a certain production level or **aggregate supply**, reduces the level of prices. The opposite policy is usually put into practice when the economy is stagnating.

Beyond the plausibility of these arguments, different studies have shown that the effect of changes in the interest rate on aggregate demand is very weak. Neither investment, nor consumption seems to be sufficiently sensitive to a slight interest rate increase, as we will show later. The mystery is that, in spite of this, monetary policy has proven to be a powerful instrument to return the economy to its desired path. What explains the effectiveness of monetary policy? Extensive research on asymmetric information suggests that there is a **credit channel** through which policies are transmitted until they affect investment and consumption.

Two mechanisms through which the credit channel is manifested are usually distinguished: the **balance sheet channel** and the **bank lending channel**. The balance sheet channel is just a new name for the financial accelerator we have already met. It was previously applied to real shocks and now to monetary ones, through movements in interest rates, which increase the information premium through its impact on the cost and availability of internal funds as well as the value of collateral. The bank lending channel refers to the effect of the monetary measures on the *volume* of credit.

The balance sheet channel

Supporters of the idea of a balance sheet channel argue that the information premium moves in the same direction as the availability of cash flows. In particular, the credit channel emphasizes the effect of changes in the interest rate among the possible shocks that can affect the firm's ability to generate internal funds.

It is well known that, in stylized form and without considering what was earlier called the *Cash stock*, we can define internal funds as IF = Sales – Costs – Interest – Taxes –

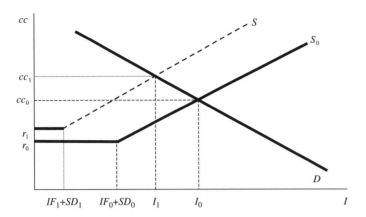

Figure 6.10   The balance sheet channel

Dividends. When the interest rate goes up, the firm is affected in two ways: (a) If the firm is already indebted, interest payments rise and cash flows go down, forcing the firm to raise expensive external funding; (b) Independently of its previous debt, the cost of external funds for new projects increases because the value of collateral falls, and so does the availability of secured debt (*SD*). Graphically the change would look like (figure 6.10).

A tighter monetary policy increases the interest rate, our required return r, from r_0 to r_1. In the first round, this increases the cost of capital on internal funds in the same magnitude, as reflected by the difference between lines S_0 and S. But, as interest expenses on previous debt also increase, internal funds shrink from IF_0 to IF_1, forcing the company to finance a bigger proportion of investment with the more expensive external funds. But at the same time the larger interest rate reduces the present value of physical and financial assets, so that the amount of secured debt is also reduced. In the final equilibrium, both the cost of capital and the information premium ($cc - r$) increase.

To fix these ideas, let us analyse a hypothetical project to discriminate these various effects and distinguish the financial accelerator from the balance sheet channel. As in other opportunities, the project has an expected value of $EV = \alpha_s CF_s$, and is partially financed with debt; we shall suppose that the asymmetric information is manifested as adverse selection and that this project belongs to the low-risk type. When posting collateral $C < (I + r)I$, the entrepreneur's profit is:

$$
\begin{aligned}
E\pi &= \alpha_s [CF_s - (1 + r_L)(I - IF)] - \alpha_f C \\
&= \alpha_s \left[CF_s - \frac{[(1 + r)(I - IF) - p_f C]}{p_s} \right] - \alpha_f C
\end{aligned}
$$

The cost of capital cc from this project is then given by:

$$
(1 + cc) = \frac{EI_{Lender}}{(I - IF)} = \frac{\alpha_s}{p_s}(1 + r) + \left[\alpha_f - p_f \frac{\alpha_s}{p_s} \right] \frac{C}{(I - IF)}
$$

We can capture the essence of this idea using the last example. Let us suppose that project L, previously financed with $100 of internal funds at a cost of capital $cc = r$, now should be financed with debt. The necessary parameters to calculate cc are: $EV = \$115$, $CF_s = \$143.75$, $\alpha_s = 0.8$, $p_s = 0.6$, $IF = \$50$, $C = \$50$, $r = 0.1$. The cost of capital is therefore:

$$(1 + cc) = \frac{EI_{Lender}}{(I - IF)} = \frac{0.8}{0.6} \times 1.1 + \left[0.2 - 0.4 \times \frac{0.8}{0.6}\right] \frac{50}{50}$$
$$= 1.47 - 0.33 = 1.14$$

The sudden shortage of internal funds increases the cost of capital from 10 per cent under self-financing to 14 per cent if half of the project is financed with debt. Graphically, we would stop placing ourselves on the diminished horizontal portion of the supply curve of funds S_0 and move to the upward tract. This is the type of consequence predicted by the financial accelerator. The balance sheet channel emphasizes the changes derived from an increase in r and its three identifiable effects: an increase in the cost of internal funds (from 10 per cent to 15 per cent), a reduction in internal funds (say, from $50 to $25) and the devaluation of guarantees (from $50 to $25). Using the last formula, the cost of capital becomes:

$$(1 + cc) = \frac{EI_{Lender}}{(I - IF)} = \frac{0.8}{0.6} \times 1.15 + \left[0.2 - 0.4 \times \frac{0.8}{0.6}\right] \frac{25}{75}$$
$$= 1.53 - 0.11 = 1.42$$

Under self-financing, the cost of capital would increase from 10 per cent to 15 per cent, but the cost of capital actually jumps to 42 per cent. The central point is that the information premium under the financial accelerator was only 4 per cent (14 per cent − 10 per cent = 4 per cent) but under the balance sheet channel it climbs to 27 per cent (42 per cent − 15 per cent = 27 per cent). Furthermore, we are able to disentangle the collateral and internal funds effects. It is easy to see that, by keeping the previous collateral ($C = 50$), the cost of capital rises to 20 per cent through the sole internal funds effects. This means that the new information premium of 27 per cent can be decomposed in 5 percentage points because of a shortage of internal funds (5 per cent = 20 per cent − 15 per cent) and 22 percentage points because of the reduction in collateral.

The bank lending channel

Unlike the balance sheet channel, which works via changes in the interest rate, the bank lending channel works via changes in the volume of credit of financial institutions. A bank lending channel will exist when two conditions are met: that the total bank credit becomes lower and that some companies cannot find substitutes for that credit at the same cost.

Under asymmetric information, many companies, especially the small ones, will find it very difficult to replace bank loans with other sources. A lasting clientèle relationship constitutes an invaluable source of information about the borrower that will be compensated with a smaller information premium. After ending the relationship with a certain bank, firms will be forced to recreate those ties with new creditors, which will involve high information premiums.

Smaller companies are heavily dependent on the bank system, because banks are better equipped to gather and process information than other financial intermediaries. The peculiarity of the bank loan is centred in the information value of the **lending relationship**.[8] Several reasons justify this assertion: first, a long-lasting relationship provides a valuable element to mitigate the repayment risk based on the borrower's credit history (the past fulfilment of his financial obligations). Second, a bank usually provides borrowers with several other financial services, such as opening checking and saving accounts that give information on cash flow movements. Third, the bank–borrower relationship is much closer than in negotiable debt and stock markets. While in the latter case there is an intermediary (*underwriter*) between the firm and the final investors, the banker's assessment and monitoring over the borrower is much more personal – occasional visits to the company and frequent meetings with the management are part of the banker's routine.

Lastly, the borrower's intimate knowledge grants the bank an information advantage over other potential lenders. This benefits the debtor (who obtains more financing at a lower cost and longer term) as much as it does the creditor (who receives a high risk-adjusted return). To be more explicit, let us suppose that a low-risk company should pay a rate of 15 per cent, but because of the existence of adverse selection it is forced to pay 25 per cent: if the bank, thanks to its privileged information, knows the true repayment risk, it will be able to demand a mutually advantageous rate in between these limits (say, 20 per cent). This special connection creates an incentive for good performance: a turn toward risky or unproductive projects could induce the bank to end the relationship, making the credit either more expensive or unavailable. As the company cannot establish these ties instantaneously with a new bank, the search gives rise to burdensome **switching costs**, which discourage moral hazard behaviour.

Two more features of bank loans make the bank more willing to deal with information asymmetries than securities markets. First, the bank's informational advantage is supported by the fact that such information can be kept private, thus avoiding other intermediaries using it when extending credit to the borrower. Going back to the earlier example, if all the banks knew that an interest rate of 15 per cent would be enough to reach zero profits, they would compete with each other until the borrower ended up paying exactly 15 per cent. However, the bank enjoys some monopolistic power, which explains the rent it obtains by charging 20 per cent instead of 15 per cent. This feature of bank loans is not present in the market for negotiable securities (stock and bonds), where prices tend to reflect all available information.[9] That is, if an investor knows better than others, the securities will be undervalued by the market. But as the knowledgeable investor buys more shares or

---

[8] This partially explains why banks are the almost exclusive providers of external financing in developing nations. Owing to their volatility and the deficient functioning of institutions, asymmetric information is a more crucial issue in these economies. Under these circumstances, banks have a transcendental role in reducing asymmetries through the lending relationship.

[9] A capital market where prices reflect fully and instantaneously all available information is referred to as an *efficient capital market*.

	(1)	(2)	(3)
Assets	*300*	*300*	*300*
Reserves	20	0	20
Loans	200	200	180
Securities	80	100	100
Liabilities	*300*	*300*	*300*
Deposits	200	200	200
Long-term debt	100	100	100

Figure 6.11   Hypothetical balance sheet of the banking system (millions)

bonds, other investors may become aware of their mistake and will start buying, pushing the price up and eliminating the gain for the first investor. In the end, the incentive to conduct careful and costly research on the company will be undermined every time the information becomes publicly available. As bank loans are not negotiable (although some of them are subsequently securitized), they are immune to such information leaks. Secondly, when markets are liquid – investors can easily sell their security holdings at market prices – the incentive to control the entrepreneur is low in comparison with a bank loan, in which case the lender gets repaid only when the project matures.

Credit bureaus noticeably affect the lending relationship. Sponsored by a group of banks, a private profit-seeking company, or by the public sector, these institutions are in charge of gathering and disseminating private bank information about credit histories and borrowers' financial information to member banks. Three effects should be noted: (a) the availability of more and better information on potential borrowers alleviates banks' adverse selection; (b) the disciplinary effect on borrowers as a result of the rapid dissemination of negative news among possible lenders; and (c) the increase in competition between banks from the sharing of information and the consequent reduction of informational rents, which in turn reduces the cost of capital. Japelli and Pagano (1999) find some evidence in this regard using data from forty-nine countries. Above all, the widespread use of credit bureaus around the world confirms that, from the standpoint of the banking industry, the benefits, summarized in (a) and (b), outweigh the cost (c). Indirectly, it also proves that the main concern of financial intermediaries is to mitigate asymmetric information.

It is no surprise that the studies leading this topic have had problems appropriately identifying the bank lending channel. The original idea is that the banks reduce the supply of loans when facing a monetary contraction. Let us observe the typical balance sheet of a bank (figure 6.11).

Column (1) shows the initial situation of the banking system, which holds $20 of reserves – a reserve requirement of 10 per cent on deposits of $200. The monetary author-ity then decides to reduce the quantity of money selling high-return government securities to banks. As exhibited by column (2), this **open market operation** (omo) increases the Securities item and lowers reserves. However, as neither deposits nor the reserve require-ment have changed, the banks need to cancel loans for $20 to reset the reserves at their original level of $20 (column (3)).

Table 6.4 *Bank loans and others external sources*

	Total	Large companies	Small companies
Bank loans	200	160	40
Other external sources	100	90	10
Total	**300**	**250**	**50**

Table 6.5 *Firm financing before a cut in total bank credit: 1*

	Total	Large companies	Small companies
Bank loans	180	150	30
Other external sources	90	85	5
Total	**270**	**235**	**35**

However, a strict monetary policy does not necessarily lead to a bank lending channel. In particular, the outstanding bank credit is the simultaneous result of supply and demand forces. A decrease in bank loans can be due to a mere reduction in the demand for credit as a rational response to an interest rate hike, a behaviour that has nothing to do with the credit channel and would also appear even under asymmetric information. A numerical example will help us clarify what is meant by the bank lending channel. Let us suppose that, in the initial situation, total bank credit is, as before, $200 million, and the other sources are $100 million, distributed as in table 6.4.

We shall examine four possible reactions on the part of companies when facing a reduction of total bank credit from $200 to $180 million. As a first scenario, let us take a look at table 6.5 displaying the sources of funds of large and small companies.

In this case, loans fall simultaneously with other external sources, and both groups of companies reduce their total financing. This does not imply the existence of a bank lending channel, but simply reflects the standard response of a firm to an interest rate increase, in which some investment projects stop being attractive and the demand (not the supply) for funds diminishes. As a matter of fact, this investment drop would have taken place even if the supply of funds were a horizontal line at level r.

A second possible scenario would be as in table 6.6.

The reduction in bank credit is counteracted by an increase in other forms of financing. This scenario is not consistent with the bank credit channel but with a perfect capital market, where companies can resort to alternative sources whenever one of them becomes more scarce (table 6.7).

Table 6.7 describes the case of the bank lending channel. Note the asymmetry here between large and small companies, the former replacing bank credit with other sources (for example, *commercial papers*) and the latter suffering a reduction of financing once no substitute source is available. The unavoidable adjustment takes the form of a smaller

Table 6.6 *Firm financing before a cut in total bank credit: 2*

	Total	Large companies	Small companies
Bank loans	180	150	30
Other external sources	120	100	20
Total	**300**	**250**	**50**

Table 6.7 *Firm financing before a cut in total bank credit: 3*

	Total	Large companies	Small companies
Bank loans	180	150	30
Other external sources	110	100	10
Total	**290**	**250**	**40**

Table 6.8 *Firm financing before a cut in total bank credit: 4*

	Total	Large companies	Small companies
Bank loans	200	180	20
Other external sources	100	100	0
Total	**300**	**280**	**20**

investment of this second group. Before examining the evidence, let us present a final variant of table 6.7 (table 6.8).

Table 6.8 illustrates the **flight to quality**, the preference of banks and markets for companies considered more reliable from an information point of view in times of low economic activity. The main difference with the bank lending channel is that the flight to quality can take place with or without a contraction in total bank credit. In economic downturns, lenders find it much more difficult to assess the repayment risk of some firms, particularly those without a good track record, with unstable cash flows over time and lacking collateral – typically, smaller firms. On top of this, macroeconomic uncertainty makes it more difficult to distinguish good and bad projects (adverse selection) and encourages risk-taking by firms in financial distress (moral hazard). Therefore, the access to credit for those firms more sensitive to asymmetric information is clearly *procyclical*, in that it increases in good times and decreases in bad times.

6.5   Empirical evidence about the financial accelerator and the credit channel

As long as a significant number of firms are exposed to the problems described earlier in this chapter, we can claim that we are facing an issue with macroeconomic implications. The empirical evidence to be reviewed in this section gives definite support to this claim.

Table 6.9 *Asymmetric information and profitability effects on investment[a], listed companies in selected countries*

Country	Total effect	Effect of CF and CS^b	Effect of q	As per cent of the CF and CS	Total q
United States	0.175	0.083	0.092	47.6	52.4
Canada	0.167	0.104	0.063	62.3	37.7
France	0.164	0.110	0.055	66.7	33.3
Germany	0.247	0.177	0.071	71.4	28.6
Great Britain	0.295	0.235	0.060	79.8	20.2
Japan	0.173	0.101	0.072	58.4	41.6

Notes: [a]Percentage change in investment to capital stock ratio after a 1 percentage point rise in $(CF + CS)$ and q.
[b]CF = Cash flow, CS = Cash stock.
Source: Own calculations based on Kadapakkam, Kumar and Riddick (1998).

To begin with, we shall use the results about investment–cash flow sensitivity presented in section 6.2 to evaluate the importance of the financial accelerator. We concluded that Tobin's q captures the effect of investment on changes in profitability, stemming from larger expected revenues or a smaller required return, while Cash flow and Cash stock reflect the influence of asymmetric information. In table 6.9 one can appreciate the extensive weight of financial factors, from a minimum of 48 per cent in the United States to a maximum of 80 per cent in Great Britain.[10]

Undoubtedly, underestimating the role of financial factors brought about by asymmetric information may seriously bias any attempt to forecast investment at the aggregate level. Furthermore, the sensitivity to cash flow, already very high in listed firms, is likely to be even higher in the case of non-listed companies, where information problems are more accentuated.[11]

Bebczuk (2000) finds a sensitivity of the investment rate to internal funds of 0.762 in Latin American countries. In such a case, a 20 per cent decrease of internal funds leads to a 15.2 per cent decrease in investment ($0.762 \times 0.20 = 0.152$). This fall can precipitate a recession and a slower rate of growth in the future: if the original investment is, say, 23 per cent of GDP, a 15.2 per cent reduction implies that new investment will be 18.4 per cent of GDP, where GDP decreases 4.6 percentage points from this single effect ($0.184 - 0.23 = -0.046$), ignoring multiplier effects and the impact of a lower capital accumulation on medium and long-run growth performance.

In reference to the credit channel, the literature seems to find more support for the balance sheet channel than for the bank lending channel. A piece of overwhelming evidence in favour

---

[10] This calculation is done by taking the average values of Cash Flow (CF), Cash Stock (CS) and q for each country, and then multiplying them by the estimated coefficient shown in section 6.2. For example, for the United States, the averages are 0.29, 0.50 and 1.61, with the total effect being measured as $0.181 \times 0.29 + 0.062 \times 0.50 + 0.057 \times 1.61 = 0.175$. The first two terms and q as the last one shape the financial factor's effect.

[11] Bebczuk, Fanelli and Pradelli (2001) find evidence of a strong cash flow–investment sensitivity for large, listed and non-listed, Argentine companies.

of the credit channel is that, for example, in the United States, increases in short-term interest rate are reversed in less than one year, but after the initial fall, GDP returns to its original level *after two years*, indicating that recessions become longer when the credit channel is at work (Bernanke and Gertler, 1995). Romer and Romer (1993) document the effectiveness of monetary policy in the United States during the period 1948–92 by showing that thirty months after a monetary contraction, industrial production was 11 per cent lower.

The postulated differences between large and small companies also find strong factual support. Oliner and Rudebusch (1996) find for a sample of more than 7,000 American manufacturing companies, in the period 1962–92, that only the investment by the smaller firms is sensitive to internal funds. Still more interestingly, they conclude that this sensitivity increases as interest rates increase, reinforcing the idea that this group of companies is more vulnerable to the information premium.

The special role of banks has also been ratified on empirical grounds. Small companies, more affected by information problems, are more bank-dependent than larger companies. Oliner and Rudebusch (1995), using the group of companies mentioned above, show that bank loans represent 39.6 per cent and 15.8 per cent of total debt for the group of small and big companies, respectively. Petersen and Rajan (1994), on the other hand, investigate the information value of the credit relationship using a sample of more than 3,400 small companies (fewer than 500 employees), finding that the lending relationship with a small number of banks increases the availability of funds, but does not reduce the cost of capital. Older companies, with more extensive bank relationships and with credit concentrated in few banks (an indicator that the relationship with the creditors is closer) display a more fluid access to credit.

Evidence on the bank lending channel is mixed. In order to isolate this effect from others, as we did earlier, researchers have focused on the evolution of loans relative to other sources of external financing for small and large companies. The bank lending channel would manifest itself whenever, during a period of monetary contraction, bank debt falls as a proportion of total debt – which includes negotiable bonds and commercial credit. However, Oliner and Rudebusch (1995) show that this ratio does not vary significantly in either segment of firms. This study as well as others corroborates that total external financing decreases for smaller companies and increases for larger companies, an observation consistent with the importance of internal funds and the existence of flight to quality. By the way, this finding proves that recessions are largely explained by the impact on small companies.[12]

6.6   Discussion

Asymmetric information is a widespread phenomenon affecting, to different degrees, all kinds of firms and countries. The main idea of this chapter has been that, as a consequence of information problems, the availability of internal funds significantly affects macroeconomic conditions as the gap between the cost of external and internal financing of companies grows.

---

[12] Commercial credit is an important source of credit for many companies. Suppliers have a certain advantage over other lenders in evaluating and controlling the indebted company, which partially alleviates information problems and could lead one to think that the main recipients are small firms. However, according to Petersen and Rajan (1997), large companies receive proportionally more commercial credit than small companies.

The financial accelerator stresses the magnifying effect of financial constraints on economic cycles. These financial constraints are also part of the transmission mechanism of monetary policy through the credit channel. As we may appreciate, this has been a natural extension of the financial analysis previously concentrated on the individual firm.

The link between macroeconomic and financial factors is still underestimated by macroeconomists, in spite of its decisive, well-documented role in economic fluctuations. This lack of interest is partially connected to the popularity of the Modigliani–Miller theorem.

A more pragmatic reason to ignore the topic has been the lack of abundant and reliable information on the financial structure of companies in many countries. Regrettably, the evidence is scarcer in the countries where information problems tend to be more severe, i.e. the less developed countries. However, the recognition of the importance of these mechanisms is the best incentive to improve the data gathering process – for instance, macroeconomic forecasts can be made much more precise and reliable, which in turn will improve economic policy effectiveness.

Bibliography

Bebczuk, R. (2000), 'Corporate saving and financing decisions in Latin America', *Economica*, La Plata.
    This examines the aggregate sources of funds in seven Latin American countries with special emphasis on the determinants and role of corporate saving.
Bebczuk, R., J. Fanelli and J. Pradelli (2001), 'Financial constraints facing firms in Argentina', Working Paper, Inter-American Development Bank.
    A firm-level investigation of investment and leverage decisions in Argentina during the 1990s.
Bernanke, B. and M. Gertler (1995), 'Inside the black box: The credit channel of monetary policy transmission', *Journal of Economic Perspectives*, 5(1), 27–48.
    A non-technical analysis about the findings and doubts surrounding the credit channel.
Bernanke, B., M. Gertler and S. Gilchrist (1996), 'The financial accelerator and the flight to quality', 1, 1–15.
    A clear and concise revision of the fundamentals and existing evidence on the financial accelerator.
Hubbard, G. (1998), 'Capital-market imperfections and investment', *Journal of Economic Literature*, 36, 193–225.
    A detailed review of the literature on investment–cash flow sensitivity.
Japelli, T. and M. Pagano (1999), 'Information sharing in credit markets: international evidence', Inter-American Development Bank, Working Document, R-371, June.
    A detailed and meticulous study on credit bureaus in different countries.
Kadapakkam, P., P. C. Kumar and L. Riddick (1998), 'The impact of cash flows and firm size on investment: the international evidence', *Journal of Banking and Finance*, 22, 293–320.
    International evidence on the existence of financial constraints.
Oliner, S. and G. Rudebusch (1995), 'Is there a bank lending channel for monetary policy?', *Federal Reserve Bank of San Francisco Economic Review*, 2, 3–20.
    An empirical criticism of the relevance of the bank lending channel.
    (1996), 'Is there a broad credit channel for monetary policy?', *Federal Reserve Bank of San Francisco Economic Review*, 1, 3–13.
    This offers evidence supporting the balance sheet channel.
Petersen, M. and R. Rajan (1994), 'The benefits of lending relationships: evidence from small business data', *Journal of Finance*, 49, 3–37.

Cited in chapter 2, this presents empirical evidence on the importance of the lending relationship.

(1997), 'Trade credit: theories and evidence', *Review of Financial Studies*, 10(3), 661–91.

A thorough analysis of trade credit as a source of funding in the United States.

Romer, Ch. and D. Romer (1993), 'Credit channel or credit actions? An interpretation of the postwar transmission mechanism', in   (ed.), *Changing Capital Markets: Implications for Monetary Policy*, Federal Reserve Bank of Kansas City, 71–116.

An original approach to the measurement of the effects of monetary policy in the United States.

Walsh, C. (1998), *Monetary Theory and Policy*, Cambridge, MA: MIT Press.

An excellent advanced level textbook, chapter 7 is devoted to the relationship between monetary policy and information imperfections.

7 Asymmetric information and the functioning of the financial system

In previous chapters we have described the difficulties a bank faces when borrowers try to exploit their information advantage and act dishonestly. We shall now abandon the view of the banker as a martyr and present him in a more realistic light. The bank is not the final lender but a mere intermediary between the borrowing firm and the depositors. Once the bank handles external funds and enjoys a high level of discretion with their use, the temptation to exploit its informational advantage at the expense of the misinformed and defenceless depositors is always present.

Unlike the bank, which has the skills and power to restrain the borrower's opportunistic behaviour, the depositor is not capable, for different reasons, of exerting the same control over the bank. The government's intervention through several instruments is therefore necessary to preserve the rights of the depositors. However, not even the government is able completely to immunize the financial system. Financial crises have created and continue to create financial and economic disruption all over the world. The origin and the propagation of crises are intimately linked to the problems of asymmetric information we have studied throughout the book.

7.1 The bank as borrower

A closer examination of the bank reveals that it too can gain by behaving in an opportunistic manner. This leaves depositors as the final potential losers if dishonest strategies are successful. Although the typical depositor is risk averse and goes to the bank in search of a modest but safe yield, she may end up suffering huge losses. Without information and control over the bank's activity, she is bound to accept the frail promise that her funds are in good hands, trusting in the professional skills of the bank to choose good projects and diversify risks.

With the purpose of getting into the practical operation of a bank, we now show a typical balance sheet (figure 7.1), which will prove helpful in understanding the concepts developed throughout this chapter.

The item *Cash and reserves* consists of the money that the bank keeps to handle the daily withdrawal of deposits. These liquidity reserves can be either *mandatory*, imposed

Assets	($)	Liabilities	($)
Cash and reserves	5	Deposits in checking accounts	30
Other liquid investments	20	Deposits in savings accounts	50
Loans	70	Debt with the Central Bank	5
Fixed and other assets	5	Other liabilities	10
		Capital	5
Total assets	100	Total liabilities	100

Figure 7.1   Hypothetical balance sheet of a commercial bank (millions)

by the Central Bank, or *voluntary*, decided by the bank itself. Since in general these funds earn no interest, they have a negative impact on profitability but constitute a cushion in case of unexpected withdrawals that eventually might lead to bankruptcy if the bank cannot repay deposits on demand. While reserves are liquid and have a low or zero return, loans are highly illiquid, and risky, and have attractive yields. *Other liquid investments*, among them negotiable shares and government bonds, are an intermediate alternative in terms of liquidity and return. In the item *Fixed and other assets* appear the physical infrastructure that makes the operation of the entity possible (buildings, furniture, computer systems).

On the liability side, the main component is *Deposits*. Deposits in *checking accounts* can be withdrawn at any moment, while deposits in *savings accounts* can only be withdrawn at maturity. *Debt with the Central Bank* records short-term liquidity loans from the monetary authority. Apart from deposits, the bank can finance its assets with *Other liabilities*, such as bonds placed in domestic or international markets as well as interbank loans. Finally, *Capital* is the shareholder contribution at risk.

Although the balance sheet may vary across banks and countries, this composition is roughly representative of a real bank. Banks possess very little capital, a great deal of debt, few physical assets, risky and illiquid assets and short-term liabilities. It is difficult to imagine a worse balance sheet from the point of view of the depositor! To simplify, we suppose that shareholder capital is used to acquire fixed assets, and that assets and liabilities are entirely composed of loans and deposits, respectively. With the following notation we shall draw some important conclusions:

$$D = \text{Deposits}$$

$$e = \text{Reserve coefficient}$$

$$r = \text{Interest rate on deposits}$$

$$L = (1 - e)D = \text{Loans}$$

$$W = \text{Bank capital}$$

$$r_L = \text{Interest rate on loans}$$

$$E\pi_{Bank} = \text{Expected profit of the bank}$$

$$EI_{Dep} = \text{Expected income of the depositor}$$

The main variables to be defined are the depositor's expected income (EI_{Dep}), the announced loan interest rate under moral hazard (r_L^{MH}), the actual loan interest rate (r_L), and the bank's expected profit ($E\pi_{Bank}$):

$$EI_{Dep} = \alpha_s(1 + r_L^{MH})(1-e)D + \alpha_f CF_f + eD + \alpha_f(1+r)W$$

$$1 + r_L^{MH} = \frac{(1+r)D - \alpha_s^{MH}CF_f - eD}{[\alpha_s^{MH}(1-e)D]}$$

$$1 + r_L = \frac{(1+r)D - \alpha_s CF_f - eD}{[\alpha_s(1-e)D]}$$

$$E\pi_{Bank} = \alpha_s(r_L - r_L^{MH})(1-e)D - \alpha_f(1+r)W$$

In a nutshell, the formulas reproduce our results in earlier chapters, where the depositor gets the expected $(1 + r)D$ so long as the bank sets an interest rate r_L such that its profit, under no asymmetric information and perfect competition among banks, is zero. However, the reader will surely notice some changes. First, since now the bank may misbehave, we allow for the possibility that the bank, while announcing that it is lending to a low-risk project with probability of success α_S^{MH}, it actually lends to a riskier project with probability of success α_s, and $\alpha_S^{MH} > \alpha_s$ – MH here denotes the presence of moral hazard on the part of the bank. Second, the bank is now required to immobilize a portion e of the deposits received, so it can lend only $(1 - e)D$. In time, the cash reserve eD will be paid back to the depositor whether or not the project is successful, that is, with probability 1. Finally, the bank may be required to put up capital W. Assuming that this money is invested in assets other than loans with a safe return equal to the opportunity cost r, the bank will pass the whole amount $(1 + r)W$ to the depositor if the project fails and will retain it (losing nothing) if the project is successful.

By construction, $EI_{Dep} + E\pi_{Bank} = (1 + r)D$, namely, the contract between the bank and the depositor boils down to how the expected return from a loan is divided between both parties. The fair sharing is that the depositor gets everything and the bank nothing but, under asymmetric information, the bank might be able to reap a profit at the expense of the uninformed depositors.[1]

The insight from the analysis so far is that the banking system, in spite of its beneficial influence on the economy, is extremely fragile. Not only might depositors be victims of deceitful actions, but also the risk and liquidity mismatch between loans and deposits makes it possible that deposits cannot be fully repaid on demand. It is precisely this fragility which sets the terms for the stringent regulation of the financial system all over the world.

---

[1] This claim calls for two qualifications: first, we are assuming that the bank has no intermediation costs (staff, infrastructure and a normal profit for the bank). But this is immaterial to our discussion. Loosely speaking, if intermediation costs (IC) exist, the equation transforms into $EI_{Dep} + E\pi_{Bank} + IC = (1+r)D + IC$, which changes nothing. Second, information problems may also take the form of monitoring costs, the other possible hidden action studied earlier.

7.2   The regulation and supervision of the financial system

Rationale

Most often the free and competitive functioning of markets guarantees the best attainable outcome for individuals and the society as a whole. That explains why governments do not intervene in the majority of markets. But in some cases there exist *market failures* causing undesirable social effects that call for government regulation and even the direct provision of that particular good or service. Clear examples are the provision of justice, security and some utilities and social services. Financial markets suffer from some market failures which make necessary a close regulation and supervision of financial intermediaries.[2] There are two main market failures.

Non-competitive behaviour   When the marketplace is populated by few institutions, there is a high risk that the cost of external funds will be higher than it will in a competitive environment with a high number of intermediaries struggling to stay in the market. Alternatively, if savers have no alternative investment opportunity, intermediaries may pay a lower return to them. Similarly, the overall quality of financial services may be undermined. By encouraging the free entry and exit of reputable intermediaries and the detection of non-competitive transactions, the regulator intends to mitigate this problem.

Asymmetric information   As they do not have or cannot properly evaluate the information about the business integrity and the financial strength of every intermediary, depositors are exposed to the risk of losing their money unless the government establishes severe regulations to make sure that depositors receive all the relevant information, and intermediaries behave honestly and meet solvency and liquidity requirements in order to fulfil the contract as agreed.

While the previous comments refer to moral hazard issues, there is also an adverse selection effect that needs to be addressed. Unlike the bankruptcy of a non-financial firm, the inability of a bank to repay depositors may give rise to a chain reaction by creating doubts about the financial strength of others. In turn, this makes it possible that an otherwise solid bank will become illiquid and be forced to shut down. This *contagious effect* results from an adverse selection problem, as depositors are unable to distinguish good from bad banks and are aware that only a small share of deposits can be repaid at once with cash. Since the whole system is at stake, banking panics provoke *systemic risk* which, as we shall see in chapter 8, can affect not just financial firms but spill over to the real sector. As each individual institution probably underestimates the social effect of its own actions, regulation – in the form of technical ratios and liquidity requirements, and eventually the assistance of the monetary authorities to troubled institutions – is needed to correct this market failure.

---

[2] Regulation refers to the set of rules decided by the authority and supervision to the control exerted on the financial intermediaries to make sure that such rules are actually obeyed. Although we shall make particular reference to regulations, effective supervision is as important as the rules themselves.

Table 7.1 *Bank capital and project*
selection

	Project *A*	Project *B*
CF_s	200	250
CF_f	40	40
α_s	0.9	0.8
α_f	0.1	0.2
EV	184	200
I	100	100

Although capital markets do not make lending decisions the way banks do, and thus moral hazard is more restricted, intermediaries – such as mutual funds, pension funds, insurance companies and investment banks – can equally exploit their superior information *vis-à-vis* investors. For example, mutual and pension funds invest money on behalf of individual investors using sophisticated financial management techniques to maximize return for a given risk level. However, they may be prone to moral hazard behaviour by hiding relevant information on actual risks and returns, taking excessive risk to increase their fees and attracting new customers, overcharging administrative costs, and the like; as for insurance companies, they may put aside insufficient cash reserves to attend their contingent obligations (casualty payments). For this variety of reasons, capital markets are also subject to regulation and supervision on the part of specialized government agencies.

The effect of capital requirements
As a device to limit the moral hazard of banks, which may fool depositors by choosing riskier projects than those announced to the depositors, the regulator asks them to fulfil certain capital requirements. By forcing the bank to put its shareholders' money at risk, the bank's limited liability is to some extent restricted. In this way, the analysis of this instrument holds some common insights with that carried out in chapter 2 in reference to collateral and internal funds, although in the present case the goal is mainly to mitigate moral hazard rather than signalling the bank's quality to the public.

To conduct the analysis, let us rely on the following example, where the bank can choose between two projects, *A* and *B*, with *A* being safer than *B*. For simplicity, we shall assume that the bank is capable of distinguishing type *A* from type *B* projects (table 7.1).[3]

The first conclusion is that capital requirements will be redundant or even harmful in a world without asymmetric information. To see this, we can check that, when $\alpha_s^{MH} = \alpha_s$ (no moral hazard), a nil capital requirement ($W = 0$) will yield the fair outcome: $EI_{Dep} = 110$

---

[3] In this case, we are ruling out the informational disadvantage of the bank. This can be justified by noting that the bank knows the characteristics of each project and knows what interest rate leads type *A* projects to withdraw from the market. If so, fixing the interest rate at a sufficient high level allows the bank to keep the riskier type *B* as its only clientèle. Alternatively, the bank may require collateral or own funds from the entrepreneur up to the point at which they reveal their type.

Table 7.2 *The effect of bank capital under no asymmetric information*

	$W = 0$	$W = 5$	$W = 10$
EI_{Dep}	110.0	110.6	111.1
$E\pi_{Bank}$	0.0	−0.6	−1.1
$EI_{Dep} + E\pi_{Bank}$	110	110	110

Table 7.3 *The effect of bank capital under asymmetric information*

$1 + r_L^{MH}$	$W = 0$	$W = 15$	$W = 30$	$W = 55.6$
	1.222	1.222	1.222	1.222
$1 + r_L$	1.375	1.375	1.375	1.375
EI_{Dep}	97.8	101.1	104.4	110.0
$E\pi_{Bank}$	12.2	8.9	5.6	0
$EI_{Dep} + E\pi_{Bank}$	110	110	110	110

and $E\pi_{Bank} = 0$. Positive levels of capital, no matter which project is financed, will create a serious distortion in the credit market, as the bank will be forced to transfer such capital to depositors in the event of failure. Assuming alternative levels of capital and that the financed project is type A, the revenue distribution would look as in table 7.2.

Evidently, as the bank faces a unjustified loss of $\alpha_s(1 + r)W$, it will decide not to participate, disrupting the normal functioning of the credit market. Nevertheless, if the bank fools the depositors by lending to project B and falsely announces lending to project A, it will pocket a gain compensated by a depositor's loss (table 7.3).

In this particular example, a capital requirement of $55.6 eliminates the bank's incentive to cheat the depositor, once the benefit $[\alpha_s(r_L - r_L^{MH})(1 - e)D]$ is precisely compensated by the cost of losing the capital $[\alpha_f(1 + r)W]$.

Reserve requirements

As already noted, banks are forced to maintain a portion of deposits in the form of reserves, which allows them to meet unexpected withdrawals. Reserves may become particularly important during periods of distress in the banking system, which could pave the way to bank runs. As a direct consequence of the fractional reserve structure of the modern banking system, banks are unable to pay back all deposits at once, since most of them are channelled to loans of longer maturity. But, as the panic starts, the normal devolution of deposits to those first in the line may dissuade other depositors to follow them, thus stopping the drain. Since during these episodes depositors find it much more difficult to distinguish good from bad banks, runs can damage not only weak but solvent and well-managed banks unprepared to face massive withdrawals. In this sense, large reserves serve to control undesired adverse selection problems.

Table 7.4 *Reserve requirements*
and interest rates

e	$1 + r_L$
0	1.222
10	1.235
20	1.250
30	1.270

However, reserve requirements present two drawbacks: first, if banks are forced to keep a significant fraction in cash (eD), additional credit $[(1 - e)D]$ will be low. This means that, in practice, reserves buy safety in exchange for credit. In the extreme case in which every deposit is kept in the form of reserve and thus banks are completely immune to a run, no credit will be extended at all. Second, since reserves are usually not remunerated but deposits are, reserves bear an opportunity cost which reflects itself in a rise of the loan interest rate *vis-à-vis* the deposit rate. This gap is known as interest rate **spread**. This point is apparent from our definition of the interest rate:

$$1 + r_L = \frac{(1 + r)D - \alpha_s CF_f - eD}{[\alpha_s(1 - e)D]}$$

As a numerical example based on project A, we now show how the loan interest rate goes up as the reserve requirement climbs from 0 per cent to 30 per cent (table 7.4).[4]

Besides increasing the cost of capital for all kind of projects, reserve requirements are likely to provoke more adverse selection problems and even credit rationing by pulling good risks out of the marketplace. As a result of these mixed effects, it is a challenging task to set reserve requirements at the adequate level.

7.3 Deposit insurance, lender of last resort and market discipline

Even with an appropriate design of the regulation and supervision framework, it is highly unlikely that the financial system be fully insulated from its intrinsic instability. That is why governments often put in motion additional safeguards to shield the system. This *safety net* includes the deposit insurance and the lender-of-last-resort schemes.

The **deposit insurance** consists in a total or partial, public or private guarantee that deposits will be refunded in the event of a bank collapse. As with other safety measures, the deposit insurance has pros and cons. On the positive side, it reinforces the public confidence in the financial system, making bank runs less probable. On the negative side, the certainty that deposits will be paid back regardless of the banks' portfolio decisions leads banks to take excessive risks (moral hazard) and depositors to be less concerned about the quality of different banks (adverse selection). In so far as deposits are guaranteed, all banks are equal

---

[4] Our analytical framework assumes that depositors are paid their expected return r. If this is not the case, depositors may share the deadweight cost of reserve requirements by accepting a lower interest rate.

in the depositor's eyes, so some of them will follow the strategy of choosing riskier projects and pay higher interest rates to attract new savers.

Also, banks facing severe liquidity constraints may be able to ask the Central Bank for liquidity loans when other sources of funding are shut down. Acting as a **lender of last resort**, the Central Bank has an instrument to counteract a bank run. If banks as depositors expect the monetary authority to rescue financial institutions every time that they are in distress, the same conflicting effects of deposit insurance will be present here.[5]

Of course, a wise design of these mechanisms can reduce the pervasive incentives associated with them. For instance, the deposit insurance can be partial, so that depositors will not be completely covered if the bank is unable to pay. Furthermore, banks may be obligated to pay an insurance premium compatible with the risk they are taking, and the system can be privately managed so as to avoid political interference. Also, adherence can be voluntary in order to make it useful as a signalling device for good banks.

Nevertheless, caveats remain. Adverse selection (again) will make it difficult to discriminate between good and bad banks at the time of setting correct insurance premiums, with the possible outcome that the final, premium may be beneficial to bad banks and detrimental to good ones. Besides, the legal limits on the insurance cover may be disregarded by the public and the banks, who may anticipate that the government will rescue the system anyway at the end of the day to avoid the painful repercussions of a financial crisis.

Similar arguments apply to the lender-of-last-resort activity. The Central Bank can establish strict rules to access these liquidity lines, namely, that they are very short-term and at an above-market interest rate, that only banks with a solid track record are eligible, and that there will be no automatic access but that access will be decided on a case-by-case basis. Again, this policy relies on the wisdom and transparency of the monetary authorities – two conditions that are not always present – so favouritism or inability to administer this instrument properly could turn it into a dangerous one. Once again, the authorities may lack the necessary information to decide which banks are worthy of assistance.

It must be clearly noted that these instruments will not be necessary if depositors exert a close surveillance on their bank's activities. In theory, this **market discipline** would be enough to expel bad financial institutions from the market by reducing their business (deposits) and eventually requiring high interest rates. However, in practice, there are some obstacles in the depositor's way. While high-risk banks have clear incentives to disguise their condition to attract unwary depositors, savers do not have the necessary information to discriminate among different banks when choosing where to put their money. Assessing the ability to repay deposits is a very complex and expensive task that exceeds the capacity of the average saver. Only large depositors may be willing to afford these costs. The underlying argument has to do with economies of scale, as most information costs are fixed. If obtaining the necessary information on the bank costs, say, $10, the holder of a deposit of $100,000 will most likely go ahead, while the depositor of $100 will not.[6] But even if the cost is

---

[5] Additionally, the money issuance by the Central Bank might create inflationary pressures.
[6] All depositors would be better off if they shared the fixed cost, but it is virtually impossible to coordinate the actions of so many dispersed savers.

paid and qualified professionals carry out the analysis, incurring information costs does not guarantee that asymmetric information problems are solved, as we saw in earlier chapters.[7]

7.4   The origin and propagation of financial crises

Financial crises, characterized by a pronounced reduction of financial intermediation and often by a massive failure of banks, have become an unpleasantly common phenomenon in many countries in the last few years. There are few economies that have not witnessed this type of mishap at some moment of their history, and more than 70 per cent of countries have experienced at least one since 1980.

In a perfect capital market, the only consequence of a contraction in bank credit would be its substitution for other sources of funds. In the real world, affected by information problems and financial constraints, the shrinkage of bank lending has far-reaching consequences on the economy. Adverse but seemingly insignificant changes in the economy can release devastating financial crises. This paradigm of 'small causes, big effects' comes as a result of asymmetric information in financial markets. In figure 7.2 we schematize the origin and propagation of a typical financial crisis, emphasizing asymmetric information problems and the concepts seen throughout the book.

The cause of a crisis is an adverse and unexpected change in general economic conditions, such as a period of political turbulence, disruptions to the production process (natural disasters, technological bottlenecks) and foreign shocks (an upsurge in the interest rate, a deterioration of the real exchange rate, aggressive external competition). Immediate consequences are a rise in the local interest rate, devaluations and a reduction in aggregate demand (consumption and investment) due to the uncertainty faced by consumers and companies.

These changes are usually of moderate magnitude and duration and are confined to certain sectors, so that they can be subdued with relative ease: as long as, and as soon as, financial markets operate adequately, those affected by this unplanned deviation can use debt to overcome it. For instance, a fired worker could ask for a loan to replace the fall in income without altering previous levels of consumption, or a manager could maintain the same volume of production in spite of a fall in sales in anticipation of the economic recovery. Although the economy would feel the effect anyway, credit would act as a cushion for struggling sectors and would avoid the impact of the shock extending to other economic sectors.

At this point, we are aware that the existence of asymmetric information gives way to a much less idyllic scenario. The initial shock accentuates the pre-existing problem of asymmetric information and spreads its effects until a financial crisis ensues. As we saw

---

[7] In spite of the partial ineffectiveness of these and other measures, we should not leave this section with the idea that banks will always behave in a reckless and dishonest way. The central reason is that forward-looking bankers care about long-term earnings, which will be put at risk if risks are not properly controlled. In other words, to be honest and conservative is possibly the best long-term strategy. The value of this intangible asset – reputation – has its economic effect in the value of the bank licence, *or franchise value.*

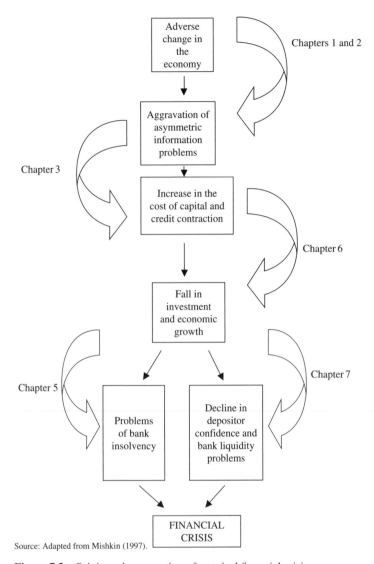

Source: Adapted from Mishkin (1997).

Figure 7.2 Origin and propagation of a typical financial crisis

in chapters 1 and 2, a rise in the interest rate amplifies adverse selection and the reigning uncertainty makes the process of evaluating and controlling borrowers more arduous. Additionally, the interest rate surge and the resulting asset price deflation aggravate both moral hazard and adverse selection by eroding the value of collateral and impairing the capacity to generate internal funds.

Financial intermediaries react by stiffening their credit policies. The increase of information problems makes credit more expensive or even rationed, a conclusion at which we arrived in chapters 2 and 3. As a consequence of these same information problems, many debtors are no longer able to substitute loans with new sources, forcing them to give up new projects and to curtail even further their current production and consumption levels, an outcome we called the 'financial accelerator' in chapter 6. As borrowers' solvency deteriorates, so does the banks'.

Parallel to this process, depositors will begin to wonder about the actual safety of their deposits. The massive attempt to recover the money entrusted to the banking system will create liquidity problems as cash reserves become insufficient. Three additional factors stimulate the withdrawal of deposits. The first is that the banks return deposits to whoever is first in line until reserves run out, so that the sooner one arrives at the bank, the more likely it is that one will regain one's resources. Although depositors may trust the bank, they will act in what they feel is their own best interests. The second factor is the bank's **capital crunch**, that is, the loss of bank capital, which increases the incentives towards moral hazard. If the bank was able to replace the reduction of deposits and the devaluation of its assets with new capital injections or with stock or bond placements, the situation would not be so traumatic, but the bank will face the same difficulties as any other company asking for credit. Finally, the uncertainty amplifies the adverse selection on the part of depositors, moving the **contagion** of healthy banks from weak banks more likely, as the distinction between these groups is not clear-cut and depositors prefer to flee to the safer cash holdings.

Financial crises, though having spared very few countries, are more frequent and severe in developing countries. The years since 1975 have seen numerous crises in this group of countries. The cause is clear: information problems are deeper. Contributing to this, in the first place, is the political and economic uncertainty that clouds the proper evaluation of borrowers and financial institutions by the interested parties. The urgency to address short-term economic policy issues also compels the authorities to neglect the less pressing regulation and supervision of the financial system: when a crisis is imminent and this matter acquires priority, it is already too late in view of the velocity with which events unfold. Inflation and flawed business and bank accounting undermine the reliability of available information even further.

Along with these factors, rapid processes of financial liberalization have taken place in several developing economies since the 1970s, lifting interest rate restrictions and encouraging free entry of new financial institutions. These reforms usually take place at an accelerated pace, without allowing the system to mature and adapt to the greater volume and complexity of operations. The acquisition of information on new borrowers and institutions implies a learning process that can take years. Information is an imperishable and accumulating intangible good: entities and investors base their decisions on information and experience gathered on borrowers over time. It is in this sense that we have spoken of the importance of clientèle relationships to reduce the problems of asymmetric information. In turn government supervisors also learn, as they familiarize themselves with the particularities of each entity, an aspect as important as the maintaining of technical ratios. When the growth of the system surpasses the capacity to acquire and process information, the system becomes fragile and subject to a crisis in response to the slightest aggravation.

Table 7.5 *Capital and reserve ratios in selected countries*

Country	Capital to assets ratio (%)	Maximum legal reserve requirement (%)
Argentina	16.4	20
Brazil	15.8	70
Japan	11.8	1
US	12.0	0

7.5 Empirical evidence

Throughout this chapter we have examined many relevant issues. To see whether the theoretical results match the empirical findings we shall now try to answer some practical
questions in the light of recent econometric evidence:[8]

(i) *Do more stringent capital and reserve requirements prevent the occurrence of financial
crisis?* Surprisingly, no. The most satisfactory explanation is that high capital and
reserve requirements do not safeguard the system, but may reveal instead that it is
so fragile that more severe regulations need to be imposed. Just to give a flavour of
this argument, let us take a look at table 7.5, where the more volatile economies of
Argentina and Brazil displayed much higher ratios than those of Japan and the United
States.

(ii) *Do depositors exert market discipline?* Yes. Banks with more capital, profits and liquidity pay lower interest rates and experience a higher deposit growth.

(iii) *Do deposit insurance schemes reduce the likelihood of a financial crisis?* No. In fact,
countries with deposit insurance are more prone to suffer a financial crisis. This means
that the moral hazard effect is more important than the confidence effect.

(iv) *Do deposit insurance schemes relax market discipline?* Yes. In countries with deposit
insurance, depositors are less concerned with the bank performance in terms of capital,
profitability and liquidity.

(v) *Do rapid financial liberalization processes followed by a credit boom increase the
probability of a banking crisis?* Yes, this was the case in several developing countries
in the 1980s and 1990s. As explained above, the link is the supervisory weaknesses
likely to arise in previously undeveloped financial markets.

(vi) *Do banking crises have long-lasting negative effects on the economy?* Also, strikingly,
no. Countries that suffered banking crises return to the previous growth and investment
path on average just three years after the crisis year.

---

[8] This evidence is drawn from Barth, Caprio and Levine (2001), Demirgüç-Kunt and Detragiache (1998),
Demirgüç-Kunt, Detragiache and Gupta (2001), and Demirgüç-Kunt and Huizinga (2000).

7.6 Discussion

Asymmetric information problems call for some types of public intervention in financial markets. The regulation and supervision of financial institutions, as well as other instruments such as the deposit insurance and the lender of last resort function, are grounded in the market failures created by the presence of moral hazard on the part of financial intermediaries and the adverse selection suffered by depositors.

Unlike other markets, the disruption of financial markets, especially the banking segment, can have multiplying effects on the economy as a result of the crucial role played by credit and the way the fortunes of both borrowers and lenders are tied to each other.

However, in spite of the well-meant attempt to protect uninformed savers, available instruments have mixed effects on both theoretical and practical grounds. As a consolation, it must be conjectured that absolutely free financial markets would work even worse.

Bibliography

Barth, J., Caprio, G. and Levine, R. (2001), 'Bank regulation and supervision: what works best?', Washington, DC: World Bank, mimeo.
  A careful examination of the structure of regulation and supervision of the financial system and its role on its stability and development for a broad sample of countries.
Demirgüç-Kunt, A. and E. Detragiache (1998), 'The determinants of banking crises in developed and developing countries', IMF Staff Papers, 45(1).
  A thoughtful empirical analysis of the causes of banking crises.
Demirgüç-Kunt, A., E. Detragiache and P. Gupta (2001), 'Inside the crisis: an empirical analysis of banking systems in distress', Washington, DC: World Bank, mimeo.
  An interesting study of the aftermath of banking crises since the 1980s.
Demirgüç-Kunt, A. and H. Huizinga (2000), 'Market discipline and financial safety net design', Washington, DC: World Bank, mimeo.
  This evaluates the actual scope of market discipline.
Goldstein, M. and Ph. Turner (1996), 'Banking crises in emerging economies: origins and policy options', Bank of International Settlements Economic Papers, 46, October.
  A review of recent crises in developing countries and lessons for the future.
Mishkin, F. (1997), 'The causes and propagation of financial instability: lessons for policymakers', in C. Hakkio (ed.), Maintaining Financial Stability in a Global Economy, Kansas City: Federal Reserve Bank of Kansas City, 55–96.
  An excellent presentation of the causes of a financial crisis and the predominant role of information asymmetries.
  (1998), The Economics of Money, Banking, and Financial Markets, Reading, MA: Addison-Wesley Longman.
  A recommended textbook for initial study of the banking system and its connection with economic policy.

8   Asymmetric information and international capital flows

Four phenomena have characterized the dynamics and the study of international financial markets since 1990:

1. Closer international financial integration compared with previous decades, but still low in absolute terms
2. An upsurge in the number of exchange rate crises, in many cases accompanied by financial crises
3. Extreme financial volatility manifested in stock and bond prices as well as in intermittent international investment waves
4. Evident dissatisfaction with the traditional economic explanations of the preceding facts.

Although these matters may seem dissonant with the rest of the book, the same guiding thread unites them: according to a recent but prolific literature, information problems arise as a convincing, yet not exclusive, explanation. Different researchers have identified asymmetric information as a possible cause of low capital mobility and as a catalyst of the external crises that have battered various developing countries in the last two decades.

Traditional economic models emphasize that a country subject to inconsistent policies is a strong candidate for a crisis. But some analysts have become sceptical about this fundamentals-based interpretation, as the years since 1990 have perplexingly witnessed financial turbulence seemingly unattributable to internal problems in those economies. The focus on information has attempted to repair this tension between theory and reality. Researchers have identified two distinct sources of international financial stability, according to the main responsible factor: borrowers' moral hazard and lenders' anomalous behaviour. As explained in section 8.3, borrowers can display moral hazard in the same way we observe it in domestic lending relationships, in which case we are in the presence of a fundamentals-driven crisis. On the other hand, as shown in section 8.4, international investments – because of the lack or the cost of information, or even the inability to interpret it correctly – are frequently small, short-term, and extremely sensitive to changes independent of the strength of the underlying fundamentals.

8.1 A brief introduction to international finance

We need to introduce some basic concepts to develop these ideas. The presentation will not delve too deeply into details that, although they would make the analysis richer and more complete, would take us farther away from our goal; at the end of the chapter we will suggest some references for those who wish to explore these topics further. It is sometimes said that a little bit of simplification can avoid pages of explanation, and that is fully applicable here. The readers who are familiar with these concepts can skip this section.

Saving, investment and the current account

We should first understand why international capital flows exist. We remember from chapter 5 that national investment is financed with national saving, intermediated by the financial system. In an economy open to the international credit markets, foreign saving can supplement domestic saving. In general, developing countries have better investment opportunities than developed countries, where these opportunities have already been more intensely exploited. This idea is derived from the concept of *diminishing marginal productivity*, introduced in chapter 6, which posits that the profitability of an investment is higher as existing capital is scarcer. In the current context, the difference between the two groups of countries is that in advanced countries the private and public sectors have invested heavily for more than a century, while in developing countries, historically dedicated to agriculture and simple industries, industrialization is still in process in many sectors of the economy. While investment tends to be higher in developing countries, saving tends to be higher in more developed countries.[1] Combining their larger saving with their smaller investment, we can conclusively infer that developed countries have a comparative advantage in the generation of international capital, since their cost (interest rate) is smaller than that typically found in developing countries. To make this conclusion more explicit, we will use the graph in figure 8.1, where we draw the saving and investment functions in developing countries (left) and developed countries (right). The saving function is upward under the assumption that the higher the interest rate, the higher the amount saved, while the investment function is decreasing as a result of the negative effect of the interest rate on investment. We call r^P and r^R the interest rate in developing (poor) and developed (rich) countries under financial autarky (absence of international capital flows), respectively, and we denominate $r*$ the international interest rate that prevails once these capital flows are permitted.

As we can see in figure 8.1, developing countries can invest more and save less than would be possible under financial autarky. The benefit of international credit is twofold: on one hand, larger investment promotes economic growth and, on the other hand, the option to finance part of such a high volume of investment with foreign funds permits domestic residents to save less and consume more in the present, increasing their welfare (although the debt must be repaid sooner or later). As long as capital exporters are able to obtain a return higher than their opportunity cost at home, and capital importers can invest that

---

[1] The economies from South East Asia appear as the one exception, but it must be kept in mind that their savings rates grew at the same time as *per capita* GDP.

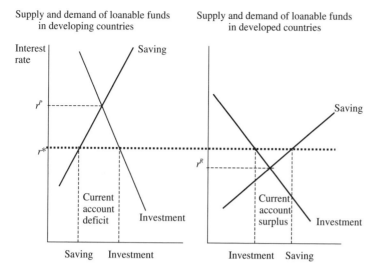

Figure 8.1   Saving and investment functions in developing and developed countries

money in projects yielding a return higher than the one required by the capital exporters, all parties will benefit from international capital flows. Just to give an example, if a British investor obtains 8 per cent in the best investment alternative at home and can obtain 20 per cent in Nigeria, international capital flows will take place – in fact, any return between 8 per cent and 20 per cent will be mutually beneficial.

The difference between national saving and investment is known as the **current account** of the balance of payments. The **balance of payments** is the record of all the international transactions of a country. We shall now show that the current account deficit can be understood in equivalent form as the surplus of investment over saving or as the excess of expenses over national production. For this, we must make use of some identities used in national accounts, the system that records the evolution of production and expenditure in a country. In the first place, the current account (CA) equals the exports (X) minus the imports (M) less the net payments for services to other countries (NS) (such as interest on the foreign debt, tourism, insurance, remittance of earnings and dividends, and the like), which we will assume to be negative:[2]

$$CA = X - M - NS$$

When $(M + NS) > X$, a deficit in the current account, the country has a deficit of foreign currency that must be financed with new foreign debt. This is an important definition: *a current account deficit is equal to an increase in foreign debt*. This conclusion should not surprise us, since it is a simple adaptation of what happens in a family budget: if we spend more than we earn there is no other alternative than to fill the gap with credit. We will

---

[2] Clearly, if we summed up the current accounts of all countries in the world, the result should be zero, since any country's deficit must necessarily be the surplus of other countries. However, because of errors and omissions, in practice the sum is far from zero.

now see that the excess of expenditure over income is similar to the surplus of investment over saving. We use the definition of GNP, which is equal to the sum of consumption (C), investment (I) and the current account (CA):

$$GNP = C + I + CA$$

As saving (S) is equivalent to the difference between GNP and consumption, we can rewrite this identity as:

$$CA = S - I$$

That is to say, a current account deficit, an excess of investment over saving and an excess of expenditure over income are equivalent ways of describing the same phenomenon.

International exchange and exchange rates

A difficulty that we have ignored until this point is that each country has its own currency and that only this national currency is accepted in domestic transactions. For this reason, exporters receiving foreign currency for sales abroad sell it at the prevailing **exchange rate** between the currencies. We will suppose that the price of internationally tradable goods, or 'tradable goods' in abbreviated form, is determined in the international market. For all tradable goods, exportable or importable, the domestic price in local currency is given by the following relationship, or **law of one price**:

$$p = ep^*$$

where p is the domestic price, p^* is the international price in dollars and e is the exchange rate.[3]

The law of one price has its financial counterpart in what is known as the **interest rate parity**, which means that investors seek to equalize national and international returns:[4]

$$(1 + r) = (1 + r^*) \times [1 + (e_1 - e_0)/e_0]$$

where r is the domestic interest rate, r^* is the international rate, e_0 is the exchange rate at the moment of making the investment abroad and e_1 is the exchange rate on repatriating the investment. As the investor is concerned only with the return in domestic currency, the distinctive feature of this relationship is the expected devaluation, $(e_1 - e_0)/e_0$ – that is, the expected devaluation in the exchange rate. Let us suppose that a Spanish investor can

---

[3] The law of one price is based on the assumption of full competition among producers of different countries. If a local producer can produce the good, he will not be able to sell it at a higher price than the international price converted into local currency, nor will he sell it below that price because in that case it would suit him to place it in the international market. To justify this relationship we also suppose that neither transportation costs nor any other obstacle (such as tariff barriers or quotas or monopolistic structures) exists to inhibit free trade. These conditions are rarely fulfilled in the real world. Goods subject to prohibitively high transportation costs become non-tradable, a typical example being services: for instance, although we may prefer a foreign barber, the cost of travel would be too high in terms of the value of the service, so we will end up hiring the services of a local barber, even if the before-transportation-cost price is higher.

[4] Interest rate parity is based, as is the law of one price, on the supposed competition between different national financial markets. If the investor can cover the risk of devaluation by means of a futures operation in the exchange market, we call this 'covered interest rate parity'; otherwise, there exists uncovered interest rate parity.

place his euros at 15 per cent in the Spanish market or 10 per cent in the US dollar market. From the previous equation, we deduce that the market expects a 5 per cent devaluation of the euro, and it is easy to see why from the following sequence: (1) the investor transforms the euros into dollars at the exchange rate $e_0 = 100$ euros per dollar and invests these dollars at 10 per cent; (2) for every invested dollar he obtains 1.10 dollars after the specified term; (3) as the devaluation of the euro in that period is 5 per cent ($e_1 = 105$ pesetas per dollar), the investor converts these 1.10 dollars into 1.15 euros, a return in euros of 15 per cent.

The exchange rate is a key price in the economy since it affects variables such as commercial competitiveness, interest rates and, through them, growth and inflation rates. For these reasons it is important to know how the exchange rate is determined. There are two contrasting regimes, with several intermediate alternatives. Under a flexible exchange rate system, the value of foreign currencies is determined freely by supply and demand, while under a fixed exchange rate regime, the Central Bank establishes a certain value or **parity** and defends it by selling foreign reserves when the public wants to buy, and buying foreign reserves when the public wants to sell. If under a flexible arrangement the Central Bank sporadically intervenes to correct undesired variations, we refer to this as a *dirty float*. Sometimes, a *floating band* is established, a system in which the exchange rate is allowed to float within certain limits, but the government buys or sells foreign currencies if the rate goes beyond the roof or the floor of the band. In other cases, a fixed exchange rate is periodically adjusted according to a rate of devaluation defined by the Central Bank, in what is known as a *fixed and adjustable exchange rate*.

8.2   The benefits and facts of international capital flows

The operation of international financial markets in practice is not as smooth as section 8.1 would suggest. Neither does the desired international portfolio diversification exist nor does capital flow freely toward the most productive uses. Moreover, financial and commercial openness expose countries to different threats, such as exchange rate crises, 'twin crises' (see below) and exacerbated volatility in asset prices.

International portfolio decisions and domestic bias
When designing a portfolio of financial assets, a risk averse investor takes into account two variables: *expected return* and *risk*. The expected investor utility increases with return and diminishes with risk. From this arises the *efficient portfolio frontier*, which shows the highest attainable return for a given level of risk – or, equivalently, the lowest attainable risk for a given return. Graphically, the idea can be visualized as in figure 8.2.

Figure 8.2 clearly displays the positive relationship between return and risk. Infinite asset portfolios exist with different combinations of risk and return, but only those that are on the efficient portfolio frontier will be attractive to rational and informed investors. Any portfolio below the frontier, such as Q, will not be demanded because it offers a smaller yield for the same risk (compared with portfolio R) or a larger risk for the same yield (compared with

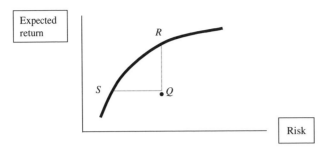

Figure 8.2   Risk and return

portfolio S).[5] After discarding portfolio Q, the investor who is more risk averse will opt for S and the less averse (willing to assume more risk if compensated with a larger expected yield) for R. The distance $R - Q$ is the risk premium that compensates the investor who accepts a more uncertain final result.[6]

While the positive relationship between expected return and risk seems indisputable according to countless studies and the mere observation of the average investor's behaviour, the same cannot be said when dealing with international investments. An investor trying to construct an efficient portfolio should purchase domestic as well as foreign assets. Next, we consider the efficient frontier formed by the S&P 500 index (the 500 largest companies in the United States) and the EAFE fund (national indexes from Europe, Australia and the Far East), a good approximation of the aggregate of world stocks not including those from the United Kingdom. The period of analysis is January 1970–December 1996 with monthly data (figure 8.3).[7]

From the perspective of an American investor, the efficient frontier exhibits the risk and return trade off of all possible combinations of domestic and foreign shares. It is clear that all portfolios in the path going from 100 per cent US to B (the lowest risk) should not be chosen by any investor because, for the same level of risk, another portfolio exists with a higher expected return. For example, the portfolio A' is superior to A. Thus, all rational investors will be located between B and 100 per cent non-US, the particular choice depending upon each individual's risk aversion.

However, as strange as it may seem, the average American investor chooses portfolio A! This portfolio contains 8 per cent of foreign assets, while the efficient frontier contains between 39 per cent (B) and 100 per cent foreign assets. This overwhelming preference for domestic assets has been denominated as the **home bias puzzle**. Before searching for

---

[5] We can use figure 8.2 to illustrate the situation of a risk neutral investor: if, as in previous chapters, the expected return is constant and equal to r, then the efficiency frontier would be a horizontal line at level r. There we supposed that, even without asymmetric information, the lender was indifferent to lending to a rather safe borrower (high probability of success) or a risky one (low probability), the first one located to the left of the second on the same horizontal line. If we had assumed risk aversion, the lender would have demanded a higher expected yield from the riskiest debtor. This risk premium would make the line no longer horizontal, but increasing with the amount of risk.

[6] The most popular model for portfolio decision making is the Capital Asset Pricing Model (CAPM). A detailed explanation can be found in Copeland and Weston (1988) and in most finance textbooks.

[7] The data from the graph correspond to the observed risk and return, not the expected levels that influence investment decisions. However, since in the long term we expect both to coincide (investors do not miscalculate systematically), this detail is not crucial.

Table 8.1 *Holdings of foreign assets by pension funds, 1980–1993*

Per cent of total portfolio

Country	1980	1990	1993
Canada	4.1	5.8	10.3
Germany	–	4.5	4.5
Japan	0.5	7.2	9.0
Great Britain	10.1	18.0	19.7
United States	0.7	4.2	5.7

Source: Lewis (1999).

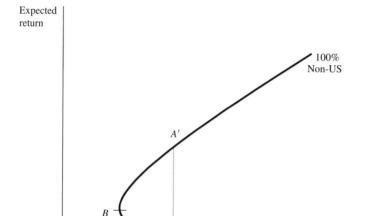

Figure 8.3   Portfolio selection by US residents
Source: Lewis (1999).

an interpretation, we must note that the same bias is present in all economies studied. In table 8.1 we show the participation of foreign assets in the portfolio of pension funds in several developed countries.

Though still modest, the values have risen as world financial integration has increased, a ray of light for the future. Even though there have been few studies concerning this topic in developing countries, everything indicates that the same pattern holds. For example, pension funds in Argentina invested no more than 0.4 per cent of their assets in foreign assets during 1994–8.[8]

---

[8] As we said when speaking of CAPM, diversification policies will be more effective as the correlation among different markets is lessened. Reinforcing this paradox between Latin American markets and the American market, the correlation has been historically very low (no higher than 24 per cent in 1982–93) but has risen above 50 per cent in the 1990s, while among developed economies it does not exceed 52 per cent (monthly data for 1958–95).

Different theories have been advanced to account for this enigma but none has passed satisfactorily the empirical test. Possibly the most practical explanation is that reported returns are not net of transaction and information costs. Taxes, intermediation costs and commissions and information costs (spent in order to learn about foreign companies and the economic and legal atmosphere in other countries) impose expenses that undo all the possible gains from diversification. Most studies underrate this source of domestic bias as being insignificant in comparison with the respective benefits. Leaving aside transaction costs (taxes and commissions are similar among countries), the knowledge of a new market has a high-fixed cost component, implying that once the initial expenditure is made, incremental costs are not very significant. Advances in communications (fax, electronic mail, Internet) should also reduce these information costs.

It is possible that these costs are higher when the foreign company is located in a developing country, owing to weak institutions and past or present economic problems that make gathering reliable information more arduous. In some of these countries there are restrictions on foreign investment, in which case domestic bias is no longer a mystery. Although in many countries there is a legal maximum limit on holding foreign assets in an investment fund, it is no less certain that actual shares are in many cases below those limits. Consequently, despite the existence of convincing explanations, the home bias remains a puzzle in both developed economies and in emerging countries.[9]

As rational explanations have seemingly failed, researchers have returned to somewhat controversial theories within economic orthodoxy. Among these are overoptimism with regard to local market returns and the perception of extra risks on placements in strange markets. Investors, for reasons still not fully understood, tend to invest in more familiar markets, passing up valuable opportunities to augment their yield or 'soften' their risk. Thus a new source of information problems appears, no longer found in differences of information but in different interpretations of the same information. We shall expand on this in section 8.5.

Saving and national investment: the Feldstein–Horioka puzzle

According to our current account analysis, an economy's saving should not have any relationship to its level of investment: as long as the determinants of both macroeconomic variables are distinct (as we should expect), the difference between the two becomes a debt or a credit *vis-à-vis* the rest of the world. More specifically, it is reasonable to expect that, as well as saving, investment is low in developed countries and high in developing countries, owing to differences in capital stock and the resulting marginal productivity. In a world without barriers to international capital mobility, the saving of developed countries would flow massively toward the poorest economies, which would experience high current account deficits. That was the conclusion we came to in section 8.1 (p. 132).

Reality shows a very different situation: there is a very high correlation between saving and investment rates in most countries or, in other words, there is not as much capital

---

[9] The home bias is especially intriguing once one becomes aware that the availability and cost of information for the company and the country are similar for both the local and the foreign investor.

Table 8.2 *Net private capital flows to developing countries, 1990–2000*

	Net inflows	
Year	US$ billion	% of GDP
1990	47.7	0.8
1991	123.8	2.0
1992	119.3	2.5
1993	181.9	3.5
1994	152.8	2.7
1995	193.3	3.0
1996	212.1	3.0
1997	149.2	2.0
1998	64.3	0.9
1999	71.5	1.0
2000	32.2	0.4

Source: IMF, *International Capital Markets*, various issues.

mobility as is usually thought.[10] For developed countries this correlation is more than 60 per cent. In developing countries, external saving represents less than 10 per cent of national investment; in fact, current account deficits exceeding 4 per cent of GDP for more than five consecutive years are rare. Compared with the theoretical prediction, this result – discovered by Martin Feldstein and Talk Horioka in 1980 – is enigmatic and troublesome. Table 8.2 shows the net private capital inflows to developing countries, suggesting that they are low in terms of GDP.

Different positions have been presented to rationalize this discovery, but the one that matches best with our analyses of asymmetric information has to do with the overwhelming weight of internal funds in business financing. Just as companies finance a high proportion of their investments from saving generated inside the company, it should not be surprising that at a national level there is such a strong correlation between saving and investment (see chapter 5).

Currency and 'twin crises'

By 'exchange crisis' we mean a traumatic episode of devaluation and loss of Central Bank reserves forced by a surging demand for foreign currency. *More than 100 exchange crises have taken place in the world since 1970.* According to the traditional view, an exchange crisis takes place whenever the Central Bank fuels the demand for foreign currency by massively financing the fiscal deficit through money issue. As these money holdings are

---

[10] Another proof of this is that countries do not have the desired opportunity to 'soften' consumption over time: we observe that consumption is high when income is high and vice versa.

used to buy foreign currency, the reserves of the Central Bank are gradually drained until the fixed exchange rate is abandoned. The agony of the fixed parity results in failure before the Central Bank reserves are gone, occurring the instant that the public perceives the excess of supply over demand of money is enough to bring down the Central Bank. This is the typical sequence of a speculative attack on the exchange rate, and until the early 1990s it has been the accepted explanation for events of this nature. In this story, the blame is completely attributed to the deterioration of economic *fundamentals*, initiated by the lack of governmental fiscal and monetary discipline.

Refuting the implications of this *first-generation model*, the most recent models focus on information problems. These *second-generation models* entered into the theory of exchange crises when economists were looking for explanations for the speculative attacks suffered by different European currencies in 1992, among them the British pound, the Swedish krona and the Spanish peseta. They were amazed at the scarce explanatory power of economic fundamentals – nothing crucial had happened in the European economies in comparison with earlier years, the only exception being the German reunification – and so the debate took a new direction.

According to the new approach, the authorities used the exchange rate as a political instrument to achieve full employment, although this benefit came with a reputation cost: after the devaluation, it was difficult credibly to fix a new exchange rate. The public, on the other hand, ignoring the government's devaluation objective, tried at all costs to anticipate the moment and the magnitude of an eventual devaluation, raising the interest rate and thus reducing the level of activity. Under these circumstances, it became feasible for the government to be forced to devaluate even if the fundamental macroeconomic indicators did not make it advisable, since the benefit in terms of employment was surpassed by the reputational cost. In synthesis, expectations could act as a self-fulfilling prophecy: if people believed that the government would devaluate, the devaluation would take place even if it had not been planned. After all, we are talking about an information problem, in which the public ignores the government's goals, forms expectations of devaluation, perhaps groundlessly, and induces an abrupt devaluation. This is an example of movement in financial variables that does not have a strict relationship with basic economic fundamentals.

Currency and financial crises have habitually been treated as separate topics, and until now we have followed this tradition. The coexistence of both types of crisis, known as a '*twin crisis*', in different countries, has stirred the interest of economists and financial analysts since 1995. Kaminsky and Reinhart (1999) studied seventy-six exchange crises and twenty-six financial crises between 1970 and 1995 (table 8.3).

It is evident that starting in 1980 not only did the total number of crises increase – especially financial ones – but eighteen of the nineteen twin crises took place in that period. The Mexican crisis of 1994 and the Asian one of 1997 (not examined in the sample) are also considered twin crises. The fact that since 1980 countries' financial systems have intermediated increasing volumes of foreign savings seems to be the main cause of the simultaneous occurrence of financial and currency crises.

Table 8.3 *Financial, currency and 'twin crises', 1970–1995*[a]

	1970–1995	1970–1979	1980–1995
Currency crises	76	26	50
Financial crises	26	3	23
Twin crises	19	1	18

Note: [a]Countries: Denmark, Finland, Norway, Spain and Sweden (developed); Argentina, Bolivia, Brazil, Chile, Colombia, Indonesia, Israel, Malaysia, Mexico, Peru, Philippines, Thailand, Turkey, Uruguay and Venezuela (developing).
Source: Kaminsky and Reinhart (1999).

Bubbles, contagion and herding behaviour

In practice, we observe that international capital inflows and outflows are accompanied by changes in the volume of domestic credit and in the price of financial assets. If these changes are not preceded by a substantial modification in economic **fundamentals**,[11] we are in the presence of a **bubble**, or a deviation of the market price from its true or fundamental value. Although it is not easy to distinguish between a bubble and a fundamental movement, specialists tend to agree that accented and abrupt changes in prices are the manifestation of a bubble. We should bear in mind that the price of any financial asset depends on expectations of future cash flows, an estimate that is always under considerable uncertainty. However, save for few exceptions, fundamentals do not change as suddenly nor with the intensity that financial assets prices sometimes change. In the twin crises analysed by Kaminsky and Reinhart (1999), share prices fell 40 per cent on average after the explosion of the crisis compared to their average level in tranquil times. Table 8.4 shows some figures that reinforce the sense of remarkable financial volatility in emerging countries.

The main feature to note is that financial return is debatable in assuming that the fundamentals were causing these extremely volatile yields. As a reference point, let us consider that in the same period (1990–6) the standard deviation of the S&P 500 index of the United States was 15.3 per cent, less than half of that exhibited by emerging countries (32.9 per cent). The return of government bonds was similarly unstable. The spread over comparable US government bonds clearly highlights the risk attributed to these markets. For example, if in 1995 investors required an annual yield of 4 per cent on an American bond, they would be willing to buy a similar security from an emerging country only if the return was greater than 14 per cent. This spread is known as the **country risk premium**.

The country risk premium is the excess interest rate over the risk-free rate charged by foreign investors to reflect the probability of default due to systemic factors such as:[12]

---

[11] We define fundamentals as the ultimate economic variables, such as GDP growth rate, inflation rate, stock and evolution of public debt and the like, that determine a country's performance and its ability to repay its debt.

[12] The factors behind country risk are actually the same as those that explain the gap between r_L and r in domestic financial contracts. In terms of our analytical setup in part I of the book, the country risk is higher the higher

Table 8.4 *Return on financial assets and country risk premium in emerging markets,
1991–2000*

Year	Annual stock return 'US dollars' (%)	Annual yield on sovereign bonds 'US dollars' (%)	Spread over US bonds – country risk premium (basis points)
1991	39.5	38.8	631
1992	3.3	7.0	831
1993	79.6	44.2	396
1994	−12.0	−18.7	1,039
1995	−8.4	27.5	1,044
1996	9.4	34.2	537
1997	15.6	20.7	503
1998	−25.3	−11.5	1,142
1999	66.4	24.2	815
2000	−31.8	14.4	864

Source: IMF, *International Capital Markets*, various issues.

(i) *Sovereign immunity*   Unlike individual firms in the domestic financial system, countries cannot be legally forced to service their foreign debt under the threat of liquidation, which makes default an attractive option in certain circumstances.

(ii) *Devaluation*   This increases the financial burden of borrowers with revenues in local currency and liabilities in foreign currency and, in the case of an expected devaluation, raises the interest rate on local currency-denominated contracts.

(iii) *Deficient judicial and accounting frameworks*   These make monitoring and liquidation processes for private borrowers more costly.

(iv) *Convertibility risk*   This is created by the eventual inability of private borrowers to buy foreign currency because of a government prohibition on making external payments.

(v) *Bad credit history*   This makes future repayment doubtful.[13]

On top of this, borrowing countries may be charged an asymmetric information premium related to adverse selection (whenever lenders are unable to distinguish among good and bad country risks) or moral hazard (as discussed below). The country risk premium, rp, can be graphically visualized as in figure 8.4.[14]

In this case the premium is so high that the country no longer receives credit – and actually experiences a capital flight – even though at the rate r^* the country should be running a current account deficit.

---

is α_f (the probability of default), CF_f (the cash flow to be appropriated by the creditor in case of default), the estimated bankruptcy and monitoring costs and the adverse selection premium.

[13] Interest rates should in fact be based on the ability to generate cash flow in the future, not on past track record. But sometimes credit history is the only concrete and objective information at the lender's disposal. Formal studies have shown that a default declaration within the last twenty-five years increases significantly the interest rate charged today. This reinforces the importance of maintaining a good reputation.

[14] We are assuming that expected devaluation is zero.

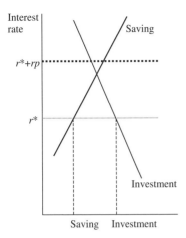

Figure 8.4 Foreign debt and country risk

Another marked characteristic of the most recent crises has been the **contagion** of a crisis to other countries seemingly comparable but different in substance. Recent cases include the Mexican crisis of 1994, affecting other emerging countries such as Argentina, Brazil, Chile and Venezuela. The Thai devaluation of July 1997 also spilled over into other Asian and Latin American countries.

The international transmission of a crisis does not have to be incompatible with a country's economic fundamentals. First, there could be common shocks influencing several countries at the same time, such as a rise in international interest rates. Secondly, different economies could have strong economic links, to the point that a crisis in one hits the other and undermines its fundamentals until a crisis in that country is ignited. For example: (a) in maintaining strong commercial ties, a crisis and the consequent fall of imports in one country will negatively affect its commercial partners; (b) if a country devalues and gains competitiveness in third markets, other countries will lose market share; (c) investors' financial losses in one country may force them to liquidate positions in other markets to cover previous losses.

Pure contagion refers to the international transmission of crises not explained by fundamentals but rather simply by changes in *market sentiment*, forcing the reinterpretation of fundamentals in other countries – *a priori* considered similar – even though these fundamentals have not changed. Although the literature on this topic is in its infancy and continues to develop as we write, several works have identified indications of this irrational behaviour.[15] Solnik *et al.* (1996) studied the EAFE index (see section 8.1) and the stock and bond markets in Germany, France, Great Britain, Switzerland and Japan in the period 1958–95, and found that the correlation of returns in these markets increases when the volatility increases in any one of them. This suggests that volatility is contagious and that the financial uncertainty in one country spills over to other ones. Baig and Goldfajn (1999) tracked the Asian markets of Thailand, Malaysia, Indonesia, Korea and the Philippines

---

[15] Barberis and Thales (2002).

during the period 1995–8, and found favourable results for the contagion conjecture. After discarding the relevance of transmission mechanisms through fundamentals, they found that the correlation of devaluation rates and the spread in public bonds increased after the crisis of 1997. Also, by examining journalists' articles, they discovered that unfavourable news for a particular market foreshadowed devaluation in the remaining countries of the group studied. Finally, Kaminsky, Lyons and Schmuckler (1999) have studied the strategies of American mutual funds with regard to emerging markets, and offer evidence in favour of contagion, as the outbreak of a crisis in one country induces institutional investors to sell assets from other emerging nations.

The fact that these funds act in unison is a sign of another apparent characteristic of international capital markets: **herding behaviour**. Guided by impulses of euphoria or of pessimism, international investors almost unanimously enter and flee markets, causing the exacerbated volatility in invested funds and returns we demonstrated earlier. As long as this change in expectations does not recognize the objective evaluation of macroeconomic fundamentals, economies receiving external funds will be subject to self-fulfilling prophecies: if investors bail out of a market, this market, deservedly or not, will crumble. 'Noise trading' is a provocative hypothesis regarding market irrationality. **Noisy traders** are those who do not act based on fundamental techniques but rather on psychological reasons. Technical analysis and the pretence of extrapolating exploitable trends in asset returns (trend chasing), the excessive confidence placed by some investors in financial newspapers and reports in specialized publications and supposed gurus – two unproductive routes to beat an efficient market – reveal that this is a relevant issue.[16] When operating based on noise instead of firm signals, these investors constitute a challenge for **rational arbitrageurs**. The traditional position in the financial literature claims that rational arbitrageurs arbitrate against noisy operators, thereby re-establishing market efficiency. However, recent contributions argue that arbitrage can be limited by the same irrationality introduced by noisy operators. As rational investors do not know for certain how long prices will depart from their fundamental valuation, need capital to cover margin calls and are required to present good returns to their clients (when they are fund managers), they may be impelled to convalidate irrational prices to cut losses.

However, we must say that herding is not necessarily irrational, in particular when information is incomplete or costly.[17] In these cases, rational investors may find it convenient to follow other investors' strategies under the assumption that such investors have information they do not possess. Thus, an **informative cascade** is in motion where, after an important group of investors makes a move, another group of less informed investors goes in the same direction, and so on. Furthermore, investors have a great number of emerging markets with similar characteristics of risk and return at their disposal and, therefore, the fraction placed in any of them will be low. If the expected yield does not differ significantly among them but they are not perfectly correlated with each other, the strategy of diversification makes it optimal to invest small amounts in each to minimize total portfolio risk. If, for any reason,

---

[16] In an efficient market, all operators have the same information and process it completely and instantly, establishing a market price that reflects the underlying fundamentals.

[17] Logically, another type of rational herding behaviour will manifest itself when all investors perceive a serious worsening in fundamentals, inducing them to leave a particular market.

one of those markets seems especially risky, it becomes wise to transfer funds toward other similar and calmer markets at that moment, since more can be lost than gained. Another alternative consists in incurring an information cost to know if the news is a groundless rumour or if there really has been a fundamental change. But if investment is low it will not be profitable to afford that fixed cost. Rather it will be convenient to remain uninformed and act based on cheaper and also less advisable indicators: journalists' articles, the market's historical performance and intuition. Finally, and no less important, lack of familiarity with prospective markets makes adverse selection more pressing. Let us remember that bank panics were the logical reaction by depositors lacking the necessary information to trust truly solvent banks. If this is true for participants in a well-known market, it will be even more prevalent if investment involves foreign countries.

8.3   Moral hazard and international capital flows

Clearly, moral hazard is the information asymmetry that has attracted the most attention in international finance studies. As far as either the lender or the borrower can benefit from high-risk, high-return projects while losing little or nothing in bad events, moral hazard will take place. For these parties to break free from the costs, somebody else has necessarily to assume them. This third party is frequently the government or an international organization, which means that local or foreign taxpayers end up being the victims. We shall how explore two relevant manifestations of moral hazard in addressing some recent crises.

Moral hazard and strategic sovereign default

Sovereign defaults are not unusual at all: fifty countries failed to service their external debts between 1982 and 1995. The literature on international economics has devoted considerable effort since 1980 to what has been termed **strategic default**, meaning that highly endebted governments may have incentives to stop paying whenever the benefits of default outweight the costs, or when:

$$\delta(\text{GNP}) = e(1 + r_L)L$$

where δ (GNP) denotes the costs of default measured as a fraction $\delta < 1$ of GNP, e is the exchange rate, and as usual r_L and L are the interest rate on the debt and the stock of debt itself, respectively. Costs include both the collateral seized by lenders and other sanctions that may be used to punish the borrower. Although bankruptcy and confiscation do not apply to governments, international credit will be more expensive and will even be rationed for a considerable period, not just for the government but also for private sector borrowers. The gain takes the form of the interest and principal saved by refusing to repay – since L is denominated in foreign currency, debt service must be converted into local currency by multiplying by the (real) exchange rate to make it comparable to local currency costs.[18]

---

[18] It is apparent that rational, forward-looking lenders will have *this incentive compatibility constraint* in mind at the time of disbursing the loan, and will ration the amount of credit at the point in which default benefits exceed costs. However, since what matters is the estimation made by the borrower, and such estimation may turn out to be elusive, in practice preventive actions by lenders are not always successful.

The last inequality has rich moral hazard-related analytical implications. As evident from the formula, the higher the debt stock and the interest rate, the higher the incentives to declare the default. Both conditions came together in the 1982 crisis (an episode preceded by a rise in public debt towards the end of the 1970s) and in some of the 1990s crises, fed by the return of several developing countries to the international capital markets after 1990.

How much does a country lose in the aftermath of a sovereign default? This is a tough question once we recognize that losses are not easily measurable and that they are spread over time, but they are surely important. On one hand, the country is deprived of the private and public investment projects made possible by foreign indebtedness during the period the country is shut out of international capital markets. Related to this, the eventual new debt and equity flows will have a higher cost as a consequence of the default's reputational effects. On deciding in favour of default, the borrower may also prefer increasing consumption rather than productive investment, which in turn reduces the country's prospective growth. Consumption expenses have an immediate impact on the borrower's well being, while investment, though offering more future consumption, has the irritating trait of postponing well being until the project matures. A borrower planning to repay the debt is more inclined to invest than otherwise since his benefit derives from obtaining a return higher than the cost of capital. Since under default the cost of capital is zero, the need to invest in high-return projects disappears.

The fact that the borrower is a government accentuates the moral hazard situation. There is a serious principal–agent problem between voters and politicians. With honourable exceptions, politicians want to remain in power for the longest possible time. Maintaining a high level of activity and employment is particularly important in getting the necessary popular support to be reelected. Debt is the most expeditious form of increasing public expenses without appealing to contested tax increases. As the debt's maturity is generally longer than the duration of the political term and the public lacks the necessary information to evaluate the use of public funds, some governments have used debt for low-productivity projects that are effective in winning the favour of the electorate. Not only opportunistic behaviour, but simply myopia on the part of the incumbent government may lead it to focus just on short-term costs, or those incurred until the time they are scheduled to leave office. And they are prone not only to underestimate the costs but also to overestimate the benefits: the default is in the majority of cases a temporary decision used to renegotiate the contracting terms, and thus the country resumes the debt repayment not long afterwards.

Deepening this distortion, the government remuneration system is not equipped to provide the right incentives for public officials. The problem is similar to that of the free cash flows examined in chapter 3, with two added difficulties. First, the official's pay does not depend on results (how do we measure the performance of public administration?). Secondly, while a business as a whole cannot free itself of its own wrongful actions, an elected official unloads on his successors and coming generations the obligation of debt repayment, without being held personally responsible. Many analysts see in this **agency problem** the root of the excessive and unproductive indebtedness leading to numerous default episodes in the 1980s and 1990s.

An additional twist is the interaction between moral hazard and foreign investor behaviour. From the equation above, a number of perverse effects can appear to make the default strategy increasingly attractive.[19] A negative assessment on the part of international investors about the borrower's repayment capacity – grounded in either fundamental or non-fundamental analysis – will reflect itself in higher interest rates. Even with a steady volume of debt, incentives to default will grow. Second, the devaluation of the domestic currency, which in developing countries usually takes place around the same time as default, increases the savings from refusing to pay the debt.

As a final remark, we must note that moral hazard is not induced only by the sovereign immunity and the miscalculation of the actual economic costs but also by the anticipation that international organizations, such as the International Monetary Fund (IMF), will bail the country out by lending additional funds whenever the debt-servicing capacity is at risk.[20] A central goal of this multilateral agency is to help countries circumvent balance of payment crises and their pervasive effects on the real economy, including contagion to other countries. Recent cases, among others, are the official support packages for Mexico in 1995 and Korea in 1997–8, amounting to $50 billion and $57 billion, respectively.

A heated debate is under way regarding the net benefits of these assistance policies: on one hand, bailout expectations encourage excessive and mostly unproductive government expenditure, and risky (and probably also unproductive) private projects; on the other hand, should the IMF not intervene the crisis would probably be more long-lasting and painful. Recent experience shows that assisted countries tend to bounce back more rapidly, resuming growth one or two years after the height of the crisis. One can also claim that, once the crisis is unleashed, the benefits outweigh the costs. While it is difficult to deny that moral hazard is present, the crucial question is whether countries and investors would behave differently under the total absence of international assistance, and whether the concessional grants and loans make such countries or others more prone to repeat the same cycle in the future. As discussed at the end of the chapter, the conditions under which financial support is provided and how losses are shared among the different players are also a central issue in assessing the overall effects.

Moral hazard and inefficiencies in the financial system

When the borrower is private, moral hazard is related more to the preference for risky projects and to the role played by the financial system. When identifying the causes of the crises that have enveloped many emerging economies since 1990, financial system flaws have justifiably received much attention. The explanation that follows fits the Asian (1997) and Russian (1998) cases and most crises in the early 1980s. In fact, Kaminsky and Reinhart (1999) remark that in eighteen of the twenty-six financial crises from 1970 to 1995 there had been a process of financial liberalization in the previous five-year period.

---

[19] These effects also apply to domestic firms borrowing abroad.

[20] The eventual bailout might also increase the risk preference of foreign and local investors under the presumption that the official fresh money from abroad would be used to repay public debt and to rescue financial institutions.

In poorly regulated and supervised financial environments, a crisis is the mysterious and relentless outcome of the peaceful period that preceded it. In the cases mentioned, a rapid and massive influx of foreign capital in the financial system funded a credit boom much welcomed by opportunists and overoptimistic borrowers. At the same time, the inherent risk in this portfolio was not correctly internalized by banks because of perverse incentives emanating from a potential government rescue. In other words, we are dealing with the moral hazard problems that we studied in chapter 7. The preference of borrowers for risky projects is encouraged by two things:

- **The inadequate banking regulation and supervision framework**   In a majority of these crises, credit expansion was too abrupt and did not allow Central Bank managers and auditors to adapt to the new volume of business by reinforcing control mechanisms and credit risk evaluation. In some cases the credit allocation process was not sufficiently competitive, being based instead on the political and economic connections of banks with the companies to be financed. Although they had the best intentions for overcoming these obstacles, improving on-site and off-site supervision takes time. More credit availability attracted prospective borrowers, whom credit officials had neither the necessary information nor the ability or time correctly to process, aggravated the situation. Primitive accounting and legal systems added to the difficulties.
- **Confidence in governmental rescue in the event of a crisis**   The existence of deposit insurance and explicit or implicit rescue mechanisms for banks exacerbated limited liability and thus moral hazard behaviour. Partially liberated from the watchful eye of the authorities – overcome by the credit boom – banks turned toward risky projects. In this way they avoided the cost and effort required for continuing with conservative policies and raised their expected return by choosing risky borrowers willing to pay high interest rates, a topic that occupied us in chapter 7. Taking for granted the existence of a deposit insurance scheme, market discipline relaxed. Short-term deposits in turn facilitated a sudden exit if the situation called for it.

Under the confluence of these conditions, the growth of credit can be accompanied by inflation in asset prices. This bubble supports a more vigorous economic expansion as it raises the value of collateral and of the bank's capital, which can now increase liabilities and loans while still respecting legal capital requirements. If for any reason economic growth is interrupted, the opposed dynamics come into operation: the insolvency of many projects will follow a revision of the expectations that will make the bubble explode, eroding the value of collateral and bank capital, and hence forcing the contraction of credit. The sudden halt will reveal the true nature of many low-productivity projects that had been subjected to superficial inspection, while the deflation in asset prices will result in lower collateral values. As soon as the government makes it clear that no bailout will be implemented, a flight to quality will take place in the banking system that will do nothing but deepen the original downturn. Banking insolvency and illiquidity will give way to financial crisis, and the fleeing of foreign depositors will precipitate the exchange rate crisis that will weaken even more the financial position of those with foreign currency debt.

The reader will have already noticed the similarity of this story to the financial accelerator and the anatomy of a financial crisis described in previous chapters. We can formalize this sequence of events. Let us assume that there is a physical or financial asset (physical property, stocks) in fixed supply lasting two periods, 0 and 1. With risky assets, there are certain probabilities of success and failure. To start, let us suppose that buyers finance themselves with internal funds, demanding a return r. All participants in the market are risk neutral. Given the absence of moral hazard, the price of this asset, $P_{0,N}$, is simply:

$$P_{0,N} = \frac{(\alpha_f CF_f + \alpha_s CF_s)}{1 + r} + \frac{(\alpha_f CF_f + \alpha_s CF_s)}{(1 + r)^2}$$

The price, under competition among investors, is nothing other than the present value of expected cash flows, and the competition among investors will make it so that this is the price that yields the required return r. But the valuation is radically different if the purchase is financed with external funds covered by an explicit or implicit government guarantee. Let us assume that the investment is funded with bank loans from deposits made by foreigners demanding yield r. The government guarantee assures the refund of the loan, which is why the interest rate will also be set at level r. The essential change is that investors will compete for the asset until the price is:

$$P_{0,MH} = \frac{CF_s}{1 + r} + \frac{CF_s}{(1 + r)^2}$$

The most interesting point is that the investor is willing to pay CF_s for an expected income of $(\alpha_f CF_f + \alpha_s CF_s)$. The difference between the price with moral hazard ($P_{0,MH}$) and without moral hazard ($P_{0,N}$) is due to the increased limited liability for the buyer, since the failure event does not affect him. The bidding among buyers will push up the price until the expected benefit is zero: if investment is nil, the corresponding profit will also be zero. In consequence, the price of receiving in the following period, P_1, will arise from:[21]

$$E\pi = \alpha_s(CF_s - P_1) = 0$$
$$P_1 = CF_s$$

By artificially inflating asset prices above their fundamental value, moral hazard creates a bubble:

$$\text{Bubble} = P_{0,MH} - P_{0,N}$$

Under these circumstances a crisis can begin in response to any change either in fundamentals or in the expectations. Two probable situations are:

(1) The project fails in period 1 and the borrower has to be rescued. If the government guarantee does not occur or is only partial, the lender–depositors will recognize the

---

[21] Let us make a comparison with the situation without moral hazard, in which case the zero profit condition and the loss for the investor in case of a bad event imply:

$$E\pi = \alpha_s(CF_s - P_1) + \alpha_f(CF_f - P_1) = 0$$
$$P_1 = EV$$

effective risk of the debt and withdraw from the market. The price in period 1 falls from
$P_{1,MH} = CF_s/(1 + r)$ a $P_{1,N} = (\alpha_s CF_s + \alpha_f CF_f)/(1 + r)$.

(2) Even if the project is successful in period 1, it is possible for lenders to suddenly re-evaluate expectations about the potential government rescue. In such a case, the price will also fall to $P_{1,N}$.

Box 8.1   Foreign direct investment to developing countries

A feature of capital flows to developing countries worth mentioning is the relative importance of *foreign direct investment* (*FDI*) flows, directed at buying existing domestic firms or creating new ones. In 2000, FDI represented 70.1 per cent of total private flows, the rest consisting in portfolio flows and bank loans. *A priori*, given that these are long-run investments, one would expect that foreigners would be reluctant to take on sunk cost in unstable countries. However, a second look allows us to uncover a set of market failures (see chapter 7) that make FDI investment a good idea on financial grounds.[22]

One reason is that, because of the asymmetric information problems involved, domestic firms do not obtain as much financing as they need to exploit their good investment opportunities – that is, they face a financial constraint. Hence their market value is below the potential one under a well-functioning credit market. A foreign firm, with access to foreign lines of credit and a solid reputation, is in much better shape to maximize the value of the domestic firm, which makes the acquisition a valuable business. Firms in developing countries are typically also exposed to a high bankruptcy risk linked to the unstable macroeconomic environment and the reliance on primary products whose international prices are quite volatile. This means that debt financing is especially expensive as lenders charge a high interest rate to cover for such bankruptcy risk (see chapter 3).[23] The optimal financial reaction is thus to substitute debt financing for equity in the form of foreign direct investment.

8.4   Case study: East Asia

Until early 1997 the economic policy followed by a number of East Asian countries was considered by many prominent economists and analysts a leading example for other developing countries. Such enthusiasm about the so-called 'Asian miracle' was grounded in the rapid and sustained expansion of these economies, which managed to maintain annual growth rates of GDP above 7 per cent for more than twenty years in a row. This impressive

---

[22] There are, of course, productive reasons favouring FDI. For instance, the protection of property rights on technological products is better preserved if the foreign firm directly runs the firm abroad instead of hiring a domestically based firm which can take advantage of its position as an insider and illegally copy the product or misreport royalties.

[23] On top of this, bankruptcy costs are higher in developing countries owing to the poor functioning of the judicial system (see chapter 5).

process was suddenly interrupted after the Thai twin crisis started in July 1997, which eventually spread to Indonesia, Korea and Malaysia.

Economists began a profound re-examination of the whole Asian model after the collapse, which virtually no one had foreseen. In part, this lack of anticipation was explained by the healthy macroeconomic landscape across these nations that displayed not only accelerated growth but also relatively balanced fiscal accounts, low inflation and unemployment, competitive exchange rates and very high rates of saving and investment – the only red light was a somewhat high current account deficit, especially in Thailand and Malaysia. This context placed a serious doubt on the explanatory power of the first – and second-generation currency crises models, leading economic and financial experts to search for new interpretations able to uncover the weaknesses underlying macroeconomic success. The one that soon gained massive acceptance relied heavily on moral hazard behaviour by financial market participants. This *third-generation crisis model*, whose bare bones were presented in section 8.3 (p. 149), asserts that serious incentive problems present since the early 1990s were distorting the functioning of the financial system:

(a) Burgeoning private, short-term capital inflows
(b) A domestic credit boom without the necessary degree of state regulation and supervision
(c) Widespread presence of corporate groups with strong ownership links to financial institutions
(d) Expectations of a government bailout of the financial system, and of an international bailout, if needed.

Moral hazard is the natural outcome of this mix, with bad and risky investments by financial institutions, questionable intra-group loans, excessive corporate leverage, asset prices bubbles and lack of market discipline on the part of both domestic depositors and foreign investors. This set of vulnerabilities was behind the East Asian crisis, whose immediate trigger was the export slump, the decline in property prices and the financial distress of several financial companies in Thailand after 1996. Afterwards, contagion transmitted the crises to other developing countries, in both East Asia and other regions.

Having suffered a severe downturn until 1999, the East Asian economies bounced back, returning to pre-crisis rates of growth. However, the recovery has been costly and demanding in terms of radical reforms, still in progress, in the institutional, financial and economic framework.

8.5   Case study: Argentina

Argentina suffered recurrent banking and currency crises after the 1970s. The last one, starting in December 2001, is a textbook example of many of the concepts studied throughout this chapter, because of its unique characteristics and the combination of moral hazard and anomalous behaviour of international markets.

After two decades of high inflation and stagnation, Argentina managed to control prices and started a rapid growth process after 1991 as a result of a fixed exchange rate regime, the liberalization of trade and financial flows with the rest of the world and a massive privatization and deregulation process. The cornestone of this structural reform was the enactment of the Convertibility Law, which set the obligation for the Central Bank to hold a dollar for each Argentinean peso in circulation, meaning that Argentinean citizens were able to transform each and every peso into dollars whenever they decided to. In the light of Argentina's inflationary track record, domestic savers began to use a hard currency, the US dollar, as a store of value, so that the legal guarantee of free conversion between both monies helped revive the use of the peso in financial transactions. However, most people still preferred to lend and borrow in dollar-denominated instruments. For instance, dollar deposits were 74 per cent of the total in June 2001 (up from 46 per cent in 1994), while corporate debt in dollar terms was 77 per cent in 2000.

Between 1991 and 1998 Argentina exhibited good macroeconomic indicators, especially regarding growth and inflation. But some worrying issues began to develop: (i) The government started running fiscal deficits as early as 1994. Given the legal constraint on money issue, this deficit was financed by foreign, dollar-denominated loans, as some domestic big banks and firms also did to make domestic investments. This reflected in a threefold increase in foreign debt between 1991 and 2001. (ii) The country was hit by the Mexican (1994), Asian (1997), Russian (1998) and Brazilian (1999) crises, a clear manifestation of contagion. Furthermore, the new Convertibility Plan gave rise to more unemployment and a more regressive income distribution, which in turn led to social unrest and a lack of confidence regarding the sustainability of the social and economic framework – in a sense, the real revaluation of the peso *vis-à-vis* other currencies in 1991–3 and the associated loss of international competitiveness added to the debate on the benefits of a devaluation.[24]

The cocktail turned out to be explosive. Negative expectations implied that domestic consumption and investment had become weak, and thus the country entered in a prolonged downturn after mid-1998. The subsequent fall in tax revenues and the lack of political will to rationalize public expenditure contributed to widening the fiscal gap. Compounding the problem, the rise of country risk, first as a simple result of international contagion and then as a rational response to deteriorating fundamentals, increased the interest payments' item in the national budget. Firms also suffered from a financial accelerator, as the country risk increase translated into higher interest rates and a reduced ability to generate internal funds in a recessionary context.

By mid-2001 the downturn had lasted three years and expectations were that the end of the Convertibility Plan was imminent. In spite of desperate economic packages to reverse the situation, national depositors withdrew about US$20 billion from their bank accounts (22 per cent of total deposits) and the Central Bank lost a similar amount, approximately 60 per cent of the total, while defending the fixed exchange rate. Decided to cut its losses, between November 2001 and January 2002, the government established strict restrictions

---

[24] A key difference with the Asian crisis lies in the fact that Argentina started a process of the macroeconomic deterioration and fiscal imbalances after 1998 but preserved a good scheme of banking regulation and supervision of its private sector portfolio. However, anticipating an eventual government or international bailout, moral hazard was present in three senses: (i) The government itself increased its foreign and domestic debt without taking the necessary steps to restore budget discipline. (ii) Commercial banks increased their exposure in highly risky government bonds. (iii) The private and public sector took on an important currency mismatch, taking less expensive dollar-denominated debt while having peso-denominated revenues.

on deposit withdrawals and international financial transactions. In late December, the new government declared a default on the external debt, a decision that could be interpreted in the light of the above discussion on strategic default: a foreign debt of US$140 billion (51 per cent of GDP, and three times bigger than in 1991), rising interest rates and devaluatory expectations persuaded the authorities to stop servicing the public debt. They let the exchange rate float and gave money-printing powers back to the Central Bank. The sizable money issue fuelled the public's desire to increase their dollar holdings and translated into an immediate and steep devaluation of the Argentine peso.

At the time of writing, the final effects of these measures are unknown. The price uncertainty, the lack of international credit, the disruption of the banking system and the balance sheet effect of the devaluation on the private and public sector worsened, instead of improving, the economic outlook. The initial market reactions and the apparent institutional damage to property rights caused by the measures adopted do not allow us to be optimistic in the long run.

8.6   Discussion

The international credit market offers valuable opportunities to improve expected return and to lower risk through diversification. However, despite more extensive financial integration, as we enter the twenty-first century, it is still clear that citizens prefer to invest in the domestic market, demanding high country risk premiums and high liquidity to place their funds abroad.

Past studies have not been able completely to elucidate to what extent this relatively scarce and intermittent capital mobility is a rational economic reaction to deteriorating basic economic fundamentals (level of activity, loss of international reserves, fiscal deficit, financial system irregularities) and the information flaws surrounding international capital flows, or if there is just an irrational component present. Most likely, all these interpretations have something to say, with the relevance of each of them varying across different actual crises.

As for policy options, the debate usually centres on government intervention in a crisis and in capital movement control as a possible preventive measure. A lot of time and intellectual effort has been, and will continue to be, put into these economic policy dilemmas and it would be presumptuous to try to address this discussion fully. Should there be an international lender of last resort in the face of an exploding crisis? The answer, according to some, seems to be supportive: the only expeditious form of slowing down the consequences of a crisis is to re-establish trust, purge the financial system and avoid the contagion of other economies through loans from a supranational organism such as the IMF. Central Banks have a limited capacity to act as lenders of last resort, especially when bank debt is denominated in foreign currency. Certainly, the decision on whether to assist or not would be controversial if the root of crisis – fundamentals or non-fundamentals – were easy to disentangle. But it is not. In any case, financial support should be tied to clear conditions in order to avoid moral hazard: the access and renewal of credit should be contingent upon the realization of reforms. Having no lender of last resort at all, the opposite and extreme alternative avoids the moral hazard issue but condemns economies to a much more severe recession and a more traumatic contraction of the financial system.

Should capital controls be imposed – that is, should there be obstruction of unencumbered capital mobility? Again, a single response does not exist. On the one hand, the frantic and unforeseeable changes in international investor portfolios act as a catalyst for crises and their contagion. As this capital creates uncertainty, it can be advantageous to keep it under control. However, controls (minimum lengths of time in a country, taxes on short-term capital, prohibitions on large withdrawals) usually end up raising the country risk premium and discouraging international investment. It remains to be seen whether recipient countries are willing to assume such costs. We have remarked that fundamental economic factors, such as a defective financial system organization, cannot be ignored as causes triggering the onset of a crisis. There will be little achieved if, beyond revising the regulations for the entrance and exit of capital, these structural problems are not resolved. Moreover, capital controls liberate the markets from outside investors but not from domestic ones who, when dealing with their money, are just as unwelcoming as their foreign colleagues.

Bibliography

Baig, T. and I. Goldfajn (1999), 'Financial market contagion in the Asian crisis', *IMF Staff Papers*, 46(2).
   A meticulous work that investigates the presence of contagion in the 1997 Asian crisis.
Barberis, N. and R. Thaler (2002), 'A survey of behavioural finance', mimeo; forthcoming in G. Constantinides, M. Harris and R. Stulz (eds.), *Handbook of the Economics of Finance*, Amsterdam: Elsevier.
   A brilliant summary of the most relevant contributions to date in this promising field.
Calvo, G. (1996), 'Varieties of capital-market crises', University of Maryland, mimeo.
   A theoretical study with distinct explanations of the 1994 Mexican crisis.
Copeland, T. and J. Weston (1988), *Financial Theory and Corporate Policy*, Reading, MA: Addison-Wesley.
   Cited in chapter 3.
De Long, B., A. Shleifer, L. Summers and R. Waldmann (1990), 'Noise trader risk in financial markets', *Journal of Political Economy*, 98, 703–38.
   A first formal outline of the hypothesis of 'noisy traders'.
Flood, R. and N. Marion (1999), 'Perspectives on the recent currency crisis literature', *Journal of International Economics*, .
   An exhaustive review of the progress and prevailing challenges in the study of exchange crises.
French, K. and J. Poterba (1991), 'Investor diversification and international equity markets', *American Economic Review*, 81(2), 222–6.
   A sharp exposition of domestic bias.
Kaminsky, G. and Reinhart, C. (1999), 'The twin crises: the causes of banking and balance of payments problems', *American Economic Review*, 89.
Kaminsky, G., Lyons, R. and Schmuckler, S. (1999), 'Managers, investors, and crises: mutual fund strategies in emerging markets', NBER Working Paper, 7855.
Kawai, M., R. Newfarmer and S. Schmuckler (2001), 'Crisis and contagion in East Asia: nine lessons'.
   A good review of the causes and lessons derived from the 1997 Asian crisis.
Lewis, K. (1999), 'Trying to explain home bias in equities and consumption', *Journal of Economic Literature*, 73.
Solnick, B., Boucreele, C. and Le Fur, Y. (1996), 'International market correlation and volatility', *Financial Analysts Journal*, September–October.

Index